SARUT

Jack C. Richards & Chuck Sandy

Passages

Second Edition

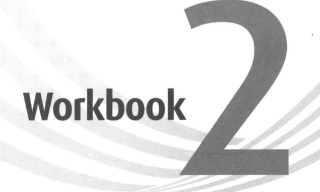

Workbook 2

CAMBRIDGE
UNIVERSITY PRESS

CAMBRIDGE UNIVERSITY PRESS
Cambridge, New York, Melbourne, Madrid, Cape Town, Singapore,
São Paulo, Delhi, Dubai, Tokyo, Mexico City

Cambridge University Press
32 Avenue of the Americas, New York, NY 10013-2473, USA

www.cambridge.org
Information on this title: www.cambridge.org/9780521683937

First published 1999
Second Edition 2008
9th printing 2010

Printed in Hong Kong, China, by Golden Cup Printing Company Limited

A catalog record for this publication is available from the British Library.

ISBN 978-0-521-68391-3 student's book and self-study audio CD/CD-ROM (Windows/Mac)
ISBN 978-0-521-68393-7 workbook
ISBN 978-0-521-68392-0 teacher's edition and audio CD
ISBN 978-0-521-68395-1 CDs (audio)
ISBN 978-0-521-68394-4 cassettes

Cambridge University Press has no responsibility for the persistence or
accuracy of URLs for external or third-party Internet Web sites referred to in
this publication and does not guarantee that any content on such Web sites is,
or will remain, accurate or appropriate. Information regarding prices, travel
timetables, and other factual information given in this work are correct at
the time of first printing. Cambridge University Press does not guarantee
the accuracy of such information thereafter.

Art direction, book design, photo research, and layout services: Adventure House, NYC

Contents

Acknowledgments . . . . *iv*

1 **Relationships** *1*

2 **Clothes and appearance** *7*

3 **Science and technology** *13*

4 **Superstitions and beliefs** *19*

5 **Television and reading** *25*

6 **Musicians and music** *31*

7 **Changing times** *37*

8 **Consumer culture** *43*

9 **Animals** *49*

10 **Language** *55*

11 **Exceptional people** *61*

12 **Business matters** *67*

Acknowledgments

Illustration credits

Kim Johnson: 10, 31, 48, 64
Adam Hurwitz: 12
Peter McDonnell: 17, 41, 61, 68

Tyson Smith: 3, 20, 47, 55
Sandy Nichols: 29, 34, 38, 42, 43, 49, 53
Peter Hoey: 36

Photography credits

1 ©Inmagine. **4** (*left to right*) ©Inmagine; ©Inmagine; ©Inmagine. **5** (*clockwise from top left*) ©Smari/Getty Images; ©Ian Shaw/Alamy; ©Getty Images; ©Inmagine. **6** ©istockphoto. **7** ©Inmagine. **8** ©Kareem Black/Getty Images. **13** ©Inmagine. **14** (*top to bottom*) ©Inmagine; ©Judith Collins/Alamy. **15** ©Vario Images GmbH&Co.KG/Alamy. **18** ©Robert Warren/Getty Images. **19** ©Inmagine. **21** ©Inmagine. **22** ©Mary Evans Picture Library/Alamy. **23** ©Inmagine. **24** ©imagebroker/Alamy. **25** ©Isabella Vosmikova/TM and Copyright ©20th Century Fox Film Corp. All rights reserved/Everitt Collection. **27** (*top to bottom*) ©CBS/Getty Images; ©CBS/Getty Images. **32** ©Getty Images. **39** ©Inmagine. **40** ©Inmagine. **45** (*top to bottom*) ©Inmagine; ©JLImages/Alamy; ©Getty Images. **50** (*left to right*) ©Inmagine; ©Inmagine; ©ImageState/Alamy; ©Robert McGouey/Alamy; ©Inmagine; ©Eureka/Alamy; ©Mark Lewis/Alamy; ©Agripicture Images/Alamy; ©Inmagine; ©Jeff Rotman/Alamy; ©Andy Rouse/Getty Images; ©Inmagine. **52** ©Inmagine. **54** ©Shutterstock. **57** ©ImageState/Alamy. **59** ©UK Stock Images Ltd/Alamy. **62** (*clockwise from top left*) ©Inmagine; ©Melissa McManus/Getty Images; ©Jeff Cadge/Getty Images; ©Inmagine; ©Inmagine; ©Inmagine. **63** ©Reuters/Corbis. **65** ©FilmMagic/Getty Images. **66** ©AFP/Getty Images. **71** ©Inmagine.

Text credits

The authors and publishers are grateful for permission to reprint the following items:

6 "Generation C Will Be Nicer." This article first appeared in http://www.PublicTechnology.net, the UK's main public sector e-Government news service.

12 "Decoding Body Language" by John Mole, on http://www.johnmole.com.
Copyright © 1999. Reprinted by permission.

18 "Technology Run Amok Adds to Life's Stresses" by Paul Gromosiak, March 1, 2007, on http://www.redorbit.com.
Copyright © 2007 Buffalo News. Provided by ProQuest Information and Learning.

24 From the book titled *Dogwatching* by Desmond Morris, Copyright © 1986 by Desmond Morris.
Reprinted by permission of Crown Publishers, a division of Random House, Inc.

36 "Study Suggests Music May Someday Help Repair Brain" by Robert Lee Hotz, *Los Angeles Times*,
November 9, 1998, p. A1. Copyright © 1998 *Los Angeles Times*.

42 "You; Getting Ready for Your 100th" by Don Oldenburg, *The Washington Post*, August 10, 1999, p. CO4.
Copyright © 1999 *The Washington Post*. Reprinted with permission.

48 "Behaviour Study on 'Shopaholics'" by Yvonne Martin, *The Press*, August 2, 1999, p. 4.
Copyright © 1999 The Christchurch Press Company Limited, New Zealand. Reprinted by permission.

54 "Fairy Tale Comes True" by Alexandar S. Dragicevic, *The Toronto Star*, July 12, 1998.
Copyright © 1998 Associated Press.

60 "Dialects" by Margalit Fox, *New York Times Magazine*, September 12, 1999.
Copyright © 1999 The New York Times Company.

66 "Distinguished Service: Médecins Sans Frontières Receives the Nobel Peace Prize" by Thomas Sancton, *Time*,
October 25, 1999, vol. 154, no. 17. Copyright © 1999 Time Inc. News Media.

72 "New Variations on Recruitment Prescreening" by Mary Helen Yarborough, *HR Focus*, October 1, 1994,
pp. 1 (3), vol. 71. Copyright © 1994 American Management Association. This article was originally published in IOMA's monthly newsletter, "HR Focus," and is republished here with the express written permission of IOMA. Copyright © 2007. Further use of, electronic distribution or reproduction of this material, unless specified in a copyright agreement, requires the permission of IOMA. For more information about IOMA or to subscribe to any IOMA publication, go to www.ioma.com.

Every effort has been made to trace the owners of copyright material in this book. We would be grateful to hear from anyone who recognizes their copyright material and who is unacknowledged. We will be pleased to make the necessary corrections in future editions of the book.

Relationships

1

grammar

Read this paragraph from a composition about friendship. Find the phrasal verbs and write them in the correct columns in the chart.

> I have a lot of friends, but my best friend is Anna. She is one of those great friends you come by only once in a while. Anna knows how to cheer me up when I'm feeling bad, and she brings out the best in me when I'm feeling happy. Whenever I run into a problem, she always has great advice, and she usually helps me solve it. She never puts me down when I do something silly or embarrassing. I guess the thing I like best about Anna is that I can open up and tell her about anything, like bad grades in school or family problems. I would never turn her down if she needed my help. I would stand up for her in just about any situation. I really hope that we don't drift apart in the future. I don't think I could do without her friendship!

Separable	Inseparable	Three-word verbs	Intransitive
	come by		

2

vocabulary

Circle the words that best complete the sentences.

1. When Mike and Ed's ideas *clash* / *harmonize*, they yell!

2. Kim and Emily have a truly *beneficial* / *enduring* relationship. They have been best friends for over ten years.

3. I *admire* / *benefit* my sister. She works two jobs, goes to school at night, and still has time to help me with my problems.

4. Jon and Scott *empathize* / *harmonize* well as a team since they have similar working styles.

5. My waistline has not *endured* / *benefited* much from Tom's friendship. He's such a great cook!

6. Lara is good with teenagers. She *empathizes* / *clashes* with their problems.

3

grammar

Complete these dialogues. Use the correct form of the phrasal verbs.

cheer (someone) up	drift apart	stand up for
do without	run into	turn (someone) down

1. A: I'm surprised that Tom didn't support what you said in the meeting. I thought he agreed with you.

   B: He does agree with me, but he was afraid of what the boss would say. I can't believe he didn't ___stand up for___ me!

2. A: What's wrong with Carmen? She looks so sad.

   B: I'm not sure. Let's ask her to go to lunch with us. Maybe we can _____ .

3. A: Did Eric ask you to present your work at the conference next week?

   B: Yes, he did, but I _____ because I have other things to take care of at work.

4. A: Sam isn't serious about anything. I think we could really _____ him on our team.

   B: I agree. Let's talk to the others about it and make a decision.

5. A: Have you seen Yuki lately?

   B: Actually, I _____ her when I was downtown today.

6. A: Is it true that you and Roger aren't friends anymore?

   B: Yes, it is. We kind of _____ when I moved to Los Angeles.

4

grammar

Complete these sentences to make them true for you.

1. Nothing cheers me up as much as _going out to dinner with a few of my_ _good friends!_

2. I like to hang on to friends who _____

   _____

3. When someone puts me down, I _____

   _____

4. I will stand up for anyone who _____

   _____

5. I can do without people who _____

   _____

6. I tend to open up around people who _____

   _____

5
writing

A Read the thesis statements. Then find the three best paragraph topics to support each one. Write the topics below the thesis statements.

Paragraph Topics

✓ Use the telephone or send e-mail messages.

✓ Be a person that your friend can trust.

✓ Join clubs and other organizations related to your interests or hobbies.

✓ Know when to give advice and when to keep silent.

✓ Sign up for a class, such as painting or cooking.

✓ Participate in community service activities, such as working with the elderly.

✓ Pay attention to what your friend thinks and feels.

✓ Get together and travel whenever possible.

✓ Write letters, send birthday and holiday cards, and send presents.

Thesis statements

1. Developing a friendship requires attention and work.

   Be a person that your friend can trust.
   _____
   _____
   _____

2. People living in big cities often have trouble making friends, but there are ways to solve this problem.

   _____
   _____
   _____

3. Maintaining a long-distance friendship is difficult, but it can be done.

   _____
   _____
   _____

B Write one additional topic for each thesis statement.

1. _____
2. _____
3. _____

C Choose one of the thesis statements above and write a composition. Use three paragraph topics that best support your thesis.

LESSON B · Make new friends, but keep the old . . .

1 *grammar*

Read these online ads. Underline the verb + gerund constructions, and circle the verb + infinitive constructions.

Internet Search

Address http://www.cup.org/friends Go

1 Naomi
My name is Naomi. I'm 25 years old, and I'm a teacher. I (tend to be) on the shy side, so I'm considering starting a book club so I can meet some new friends. I (plan to start) this club as soon as possible, so e-mail me if you're interested! Naomi247@cup.org

2 Renee
I just moved here, and I'm looking for some new friends. I appreciate spending evenings at home cooking and listening to music. People say I tend to be kind of quiet, but I'm fun once you get to know me. If you enjoy sharing recipes, e-mail me. Renee8334@cup.org

3 Alex
I'm Alex Ramirez, an engineering student at National University. I love biking. Can I suggest starting a bikers' meet-up group? I'm considering entering a race and therefore I intend to start riding my bike every day. I hope others will join me! aramirez@cup.org

2 *grammar*

Complete the questions using the gerund or infinitive form of the verbs. Note that one of the constructions uses the passive voice. Then answer the questions and give reasons.

1. Do you get annoyed when friends ask ____to borrow____ (borrow) your CDs or clothes?

   No, I don't get annoyed when friends ask to borrow my CDs or clothes
   because I know they will return them.

2. Would you consider _____ (share) an apartment with a friend?

3. Would you refuse _____ (go out) with a friend if he or she wanted to see a movie you weren't interested in seeing?

4. Do you expect _____ (invite) every time your best friend goes out?

5. Which friend do you prefer _____ (hang out) with the most?

6. When a friend treats you to lunch, do you enjoy _____ (go) to a casual restaurant or a more formal one?

7. Would you continue _____ (talk) to a friend if she never returned your phone calls or answered your e-mails?

vocabulary

Circle the words that best complete the sentences.

1. Maria and Emma *rekindled / resurfaced* their friendship after drifting apart from each other for many years.

2. My family *reunion / resurface* is next month. I can't wait to see all my relatives!

3. Too much damage has happened to Al and Sam's friendship to *redefine / rebuild* it.

4. I can't *rehash / recall* the name of my tenth-grade English teacher.

5. Tim has *reconnected / redefined* his outlook on life. He's more optimistic now.

6. Don't bring that subject up again. I don't want to *rehash / rebuild* it with you.

7. After studying for the exam for two days, Cara *redefined / resurfaced* to eat dinner with her family.

8. I'm glad I came home for spring break. I've been *recalling / reconnecting* with friends that I haven't seen since last summer.

grammar

Imagine your friend is coming to visit you for the weekend. Write sentences describing each possible activity you can do together. Use the cues and the gerund or infinitive form of the verbs given.

1. plan / take a walk by the lake

   We should plan to take a walk
   by the lake.
   _____

2. suggest / eat dinner at a French café

   _____
   _____

3. consider / go to a karaoke club

   _____
   _____
   _____

4. prefer / get tickets to a concert

   _____
   _____
   _____

5

reading

A Read the article. Find the words in boldface that match the definitions.

1. the ideas contained in something written or spoken _____content_____

2. to join together as one _____

3. between 45 and 65 years old _____

4. the quality of having unclear boundaries _____

5. a way that someone typically behaves _____

Generation C will be nicer

Tomorrow's generation, or "Generation C," will be nicer, according to a report by the Social Issues Research Centre of Oxford, England. The study was undertaken to examine how the Internet is shaping our lives. It predicts that Generation C (standing for **content**, connectivity, creativity, collaboration, and communication) will be nicer to each other and more able to communicate with a wider variety of people.

Generation C, whose members will be **middle aged** by 2020, will have grown up under the Internet's principles of cooperation, exchange, and sharing of information. This knowledge will have strong yet positive consequences for society. The study also predicts a future with a greater **blurring** of real and virtual worlds, where the Internet and computer technology will continue to blend into our daily lives to become a norm for everyone.

The study points out that the number of social networking sites is increasing rapidly. These include those that cater to special-interest groups and those that **unite** people separated by geography. These sites are important because online relationships tend to be formed with people we do not normally come into contact with during our daily lives. This contact can broaden our horizons and increase understanding and tolerance among people from different backgrounds.

Although there is a **tendency** to focus on the Internet's negative implications, this study suggests that while there will still be problems, a more positive future lies ahead.

B Check (✓) the statements the author would probably agree with.

☐ 1. Generation C will only be able to communicate with younger people.

☐ 2. Generation C people could have friends all over the world.

☐ 3. Good things will come of Generation C's ability to cooperate.

☐ 4. Computing and technology will be a part of everyone's daily lives.

☐ 5. Generation C will have problems making friends online.

LESSON A · The way we dress

grammar

Match the sentences to tell the story of Mimi, a fashion designer in Tokyo.

Mimi's Story

1. When I was a small child, I enjoyed __i__
2. As I got a little older, I wanted to __g__
3. When I was a teenager, my parents permitted __d__
4. My mother recognized my interest in clothing, and she encouraged __e__
5. By the time I graduated from high school, I knew that I wanted __h__
6. My teachers advised __b__
7. I thought that the high cost of the school would prevent __c__
8. Fortunately, I got a scholarship that allowed __f__
9. Now, five years after graduating, I'm a fashion designer. I love __a__

a. designing beautiful clothes for the best shops!
b. going to a fashion school in New York City.
c. me from going there.
d. me to wear the clothes I liked.
e. me to learn more about it.
f. me to study there for four years.
g. make my own choices about what to wear.
h. to work in the fashion industry.
i. wearing what my mother bought me.

vocabulary

Circle the words that best complete the sentences.

1. People read fashion magazines to learn about the *sloppy* / *stylish* new clothing for each season.

2. If you are planning to go to a fancy club, wear something *chic* / *functional*.

3. Marco's *conservative* / *flashy* suit looked good for his interview at the bank.

4. Most teenagers think adults wear unimaginative, *fashionable* / *stuffy* clothing.

5. When I'm alone at home, I can wear *formal* / *sloppy* clothes if I want.

6. I can't believe my friends are wearing *retro* / *trendy* clothes from the 1980s.

7. When I'm gardening, I wear *flashy* / *functional* jeans and a T-shirt.

8. Pop stars often wear *funky* / *stuffy* clothes on stage.

3

grammar

Read the blog post about clothes and fashion. Use the gerund or the infinitive form of the verbs in parentheses.

Fashion Statements

If you ask me, I think people are just trying **1** ___to impress___ (impress) other people when they wear expensive clothes. I don't mind when people wear stylish clothing – I just think they tend **2** _____ (put) too much emphasis on designer labels. I think most people should try **3** _____ (look) neat and well dressed, but give up **4** _____ (buy) designer clothing. There are too many serious problems in the world. I mean, just reading stories about poverty in the newspaper encourages me **5** _____ (avoid) expensive clothing stores. I want to discourage people from **6** _____ (spend) money on luxuries like fancy clothes. Instead, I want to encourage them **7** _____ (donate) more of their money to charity. People might tend **8** _____ (feel) better about themselves if they knew their money was helping someone who truly needed it.

💬 COMMENTS (3)

4

grammar

Complete these sentences to make them true for you.

1. I don't mind wearing clothes that _are handed down to me from my brothers or cousins._

2. I hate to wear clothes that _____

3. I love to wear clothes that _____

4. I tend to buy clothes _____

5. I don't think parents should allow teenagers to wear _____

writing

A Underline the thesis statements in these introductory paragraphs. Then complete the paragraphs that follow with examples supporting each thesis statement.

Getting dressed up can be a lot of fun if you have the right attitude. Many people despise dressing up and can't wait to get back into their jeans and sweatshirts, but I love putting on my best clothes. I plan what I am going to wear very carefully. I like to dress nicely for many different types of occasions. For example, _____

_____

_____

There are many advantages to dressing nicely. For example, _____

_____

_____

Teenagers spend a significant portion of their income on the "right clothes." For example, following the newest trends in an effort to fit in can become an obsession. I feel that young people need to reject pressure to dress stylishly. Keeping up with the latest fashions is an expensive pursuit. For example, _____

_____

_____

Television and fashion magazines do not set a good example. That is, _____

_____

_____

B Choose one of these topics to write about. Write a thesis statement that expresses your own point of view.

1. There *are / aren't* many advantages to dressing casually at work.

2. Teenagers *should / shouldn't* be required to wear school uniforms.

3. Employees *should / shouldn't* be judged by what they wear.

C Make a list of examples that support your thesis statement.

_____

_____

_____

D Use your thesis statement and examples to develop a composition containing an introductory paragraph and at least two supporting paragraphs.

grammar

Read the e-mail and underline the cleft sentences.

File   Edit   View   Help

To: Beth
Subject: My Brother

Dear Beth,

Guess what? My brother Kyle visited me. I haven't seen him in a year. What I noticed first was the three inches he grew. He's doing well in school, and he has a part-time job at a supermarket. He wanted to go out to lunch, so we went to my favorite café. He told me he is saving money for college. What struck me most about my brother was how grown-up he seemed. After lunch we walked through the park. Then he had to leave, but before he did, he gave me a big hug and promised to visit me again. What I realized at the end of the visit was that I have a really terrific brother!

Love, Erica

grammar

Read what each person thought about Gina Riccardi, the model who visited an advertising agency. Then complete the dialogue using cleft sentences with *noticed, liked, admired,* or *struck me.*

Jin: She's as beautiful in person as she is in her ads.

Brian: She is gorgeous, but (1) _what I noticed first was that beautiful dress!_

Dolores: Not me. (2) _____

How about you, Jin?

Jin: Yes, her eyes are stunning, but (3) _____

Ted: As for me, (4) _____

Brian: Her voice? Come on, Ted. She's a fashion model, not a singer!

vocabulary

Choose the words that best complete the sentences.

arrogant	innocent	intense	sympathetic
eccentric	intellectual	sinister	trustworthy

1. People think Liz is strange and _____eccentric_____ because she lives with 12 cats.

2. The villain's small eyes gave him an evil and _____ look.

3. My boss is so _____ . He thinks he's better than everyone in the office.

4. If you need a _____ person to talk to, try Maya. She's very understanding.

5. Don't count on Jiro to complete his part of the project. He's not very _____ .

6. No wonder Ted won the tennis match. He was so _____ and focused.

7. Keri is so _____ . She could be a college professor!

8. Guy pretends to be _____ , but I heard he has a wild and crazy side.

grammar

Imagine you are hiring a new employee. What personal characteristics do you look for? Use your own ideas to complete these sentences.

1. What I look for in an employee is *a strong dedication to the company.* _____

_____

2. What I think is most important is _____

_____

3. What I probably notice first is _____

_____

4. What I pay attention to is _____

_____

5. What I ask about first is _____

_____

6. What I think is least important is _____

_____

5

reading

A Read the article on body language quickly. What qualities do you think might apply to each body language type?

	Willing to listen	Not willing to listen	Engaged in conversation	Not engaged in conversation
1. responsive	☐	☐	☐	☐
2. reflective	☐	☐	☐	☐
3. combative	☐	☐	☐	☐
4. fugitive	☐	☐	☐	☐

Understanding Body Language

In European and North American cultures, body language behaviors can be divided into two groups: open/closed and forward/back.

Open/closed postures are the easiest to recognize. People are open to messages when they show open hands, face you fully, and have both feet on the ground. This indicates that they are willing to listen to what you have to say, even if they are disagreeing with you. When people are closed to messages, they have their arms folded or their legs crossed, and they may turn their bodies away. What this body language usually means is that people are rejecting your message.

Forward/back behavior reveals an active or a passive reaction to what is being said. If people lean forward with their bodies toward you, they are actively engaged in your message. They may be accepting or rejecting it, but their minds are on what you are saying. On the other hand, if people lean back in their chairs or look away from you, or perform activities such as drawing or cleaning their eyeglasses, you know that they are either passively taking in your message or that they are ignoring it. In either case, they are not very much engaged in the conversation.

The chart below shows how these types of body language can suggest the general mental state of the listener.

OPEN

RESPONSIVE: The person is willing to listen to you (open) and wants to participate in the conversation (forward).

REFLECTIVE: The person is willing to listen (open) but not to share his or her opinion (back). He or she wants more time to think.

FORWARD · · · · · · · · · · · · · · · · **BACK**

COMBATIVE: There is risk of an argument. The person is engaged in the conversation (forward) but rejects your message (closed).

FUGITIVE: The person is trying to avoid the conversation. He or she does not want to be a part of the conversation (back) and is rejecting your message (closed).

CLOSED

B Write the body language type under each picture.

responsive
reflective
combative
fugitive

_____ _____ _____ _____

3 Science and technology

LESSON A · Good science, bad science

1

grammar

Check the sentences that use articles incorrectly, and then rewrite them.

☑ 1. For many people, using an abacus is an alternative to using calculator.

For many people, using an abacus is an alternative to using a calculator.

☐ 2. Abacus is the earliest form of mechanical computing.

_____

☐ 3. The abacus was invented more than 5,000 years ago.

_____

☐ 4. It consists of wooden frame with wires that are strung together.

_____

☐ 5. An abacus usually has 13 wires. On wires are beads, which represent units.

_____

☐ 6. Calculations are made by moving the beads up and down.

_____

☐ 7. Skilled operator can make calculations on it very quickly.

_____

2

vocabulary

Choose the words that best complete the sentences.

audacious	frivolous	problematic	unethical
confidential	hazardous	prudent	

1. Plastic surgery can be harmful and a ____frivolous____ waste of money.
2. Curing cancer is still a ____problematic____ issue for scientists.
3. In some countries, doctors must keep medical records ____confidential____ . They are forbidden to share information, even with family members.
4. Some people get sick due to improper storage or disposal of ____hazardous____ materials like chemicals and poisons.
5. It's illegal and ____unethical____ to download music without paying for it.
6. It will take ____audacious____ actions to go against the boss's plans.
7. Be ____prudent____ before signing the contract. Don't put yourself at risk by making a bad deal.

grammar

Complete the text with *a*, *an*, or *the*. Put an **X** where an article is not required.

Digital Cameras

(1) __The__ digital camera has changed the way we take (2) ___x___ pictures. As with most technology, there are advantages and drawbacks to digital cameras.

Traditional cameras work by focusing (3) __an__ image onto light-sensitive film in the camera. To see the pictures, you have to send (4) __the__ film to (5) __a__ company that processes it. This is (6) __a__ process that can take several days.

Digital Camera

Digital cameras don't use film. Rather, they convert light entering the camera into (7) __x__ information that can be read by (8) __a__ computer.

Then you can also post your pictures on the Internet. Another advantage of (9) _____ digital cameras is that you can see your work immediately. If you don't like (10) __a, the__ picture, you can simply erase it by pressing (11) __a__ button.

grammar

Write a sentence about each topic.
• the trendiest product on the market
• the most helpful kind of technology invented
• the silliest invention
• a medical cure I'd like to see discovered
• the most interesting website

1. I think the trendiest product on the market is the plasma TV.

2. _____

_____

3. _____

_____

4. _____

_____

5. _____

_____

5

writing

A   Read the article. Underline the information in each paragraph that would belong in a summary.

PAY ONLINE AND $AVE!

It's probably happened to you at some point. You look at the calendar and realize your car insurance bill is due tomorrow, and you've forgotten to pay it. Now, because your payment will be late, you risk incurring a late fee or even having your insurance canceled. Relax! With advances in computer technology, you can pay your bills online and on time.

It's relatively easy to open an electronic bill-paying account. Most banks offer confidential services, usually with little or no fee. If your bank doesn't offer electronic bill-paying services, you can set up an electronic account with a third-party Internet service, or you can set up individual electronic accounts with your billers – the electric company, department stores, the phone company, and so on.

Once you establish your electronic account, you can decide when and who to pay by

simply filling in the proper account information. If you prefer to initiate the payments yourself, you can tell your account to make a payment immediately (like that car insurance payment that is due tomorrow). Or, you can set your account up to pay your bills automatically. If your water bill is due on the 15th of each month, you can instruct your account to transfer the amount you owe to the water company on the 14th of each month.

One of the most surprising benefits of online bill paying is that you're helping the environment. By paying bills online, you save trees by not using paper bills and envelopes. You also help cut back on air pollution because your bill doesn't need to be carried by trucks or airplanes. It is estimated that 1.6 billion tons of solid waste could be eliminated if the U.S. population paid its bills online.

B   Check (✓) the sentence in each pair that could belong in a summary of the passage.

1. ☐ There are a number of convenient ways to set up an electronic bill-paying account.
    ☐ Some third-party e-billing companies charge about $5 for every 12 payments you make using their services.

2. ☐ Not only do you benefit from paying bills online by reducing your stress, the environment benefits as well.
    ☐ If everyone pays their bills online, greenhouse-gas emissions will be reduced by 2.1 million tons each year.

C   Now write a summary of the passage.

_____

_____

_____

_____

LESSON B · Technology and you

1 grammar

Read the sentences. Check (✓) the -ing clause that implies actions that happened at the same time, at a different time, or for a reason.

	Same time	Different time	Reason
1. Having recently learned how to text-message, Ally now texts me four to five times a day!	☐	✓	☐
2. Being a prudent consumer, I did research before I bought my laptop.	☐	☐	☑
3. While driving to work last week, my car overheated.	☑	☐	☐
4. Having lost my ATM card, I can't withdraw money from ATM machines.	☐	☐	☑
5. Having set up my new Internet phone account, I can now make calls to anywhere for free.	☐	☑	☐
6. Zoe is in her room watching a flat screen TV.	☑	☐	☐
7. Having had trouble programming the DVR, I now ask my kids to program it for me.	☐	☐	☑

2 grammar

Write sentences using the cues and an -ing clause.

1. *Same time:* Lily / break her digital camera / take a picture
   Lily broke her digital camera taking a picture.
   Taking a picture, Lily broke her digital camera.

2. *Different time:* Diego / watch a show about alternative energy / buy a hybrid car

3. *Reason:* Bella / be a resourceful person / build her own computer

4. *Different time:* Dan / download too many files / crash his laptop

5. *Same time:* Celia / be in her car / listen to satellite radio

6. *Reason:* Ken / be an adventurous person / sign up for an eco-adventure tour in Belize

vocabulary

Match the phrases to make logical sentences.

1. Anita is fed up with Isaac __c__
2. Children are reliant on their parents __f__
3. Julia is grateful for all the help __a__
4. Be very familiar with __h__
5. I'm curious about __g__
6. People are intimidated by George, __e__
7. Gwen is so crazy about cooking __d__
8. I've been suspicious of Ryan __b__

a. she got from friends while she was ill.
b. ever since I saw him eating my lunch.
c. because he asks too many questions.
d. that she opened her own restaurant.
e. but he's actually nicer than he looks!
f. to feed, shelter, and clothe them until they're grown.
g. what happens next on my favorite TV show.
h. the subject matter in the unit before you take the test.

grammar

Have you had good or bad experiences with the new technology in the box?
Write sentences about your experience using *-ing* clauses.

> using a digital camera
> looking for information online
> learning how to use a new cell phone
> buying airline tickets online

1. Having bought a new digital camera, I realized I didn't know how to use it.

2. _____

3. _____

4. _____

A What does *run amok* mean in the title of the reading text? Read the blog and check (✓) your answer.

☐ going too fast ☐ going wild and out of control ☐ giving too much information

http://www.cambridge.org/technologyrunamok

News ▾

Technology Run Amok Adds to Life's Stresses

I have accepted my share of technology in my daily life. What concerns me is how rapidly technology seems to be taking complete control of our lives. Once our servant, I think technology is now our master.

For example, the distribution of information, once carefully researched, is now completely uncontrolled on the Internet. Anyone can say anything and nobody has the time to weed out truth from fiction. There is a vast ocean of just words and opinions online. When I go to the local library, at least I know I can trust the librarian to direct me to the best information available on any topic. The Internet is full of "authorities" whose credentials are questionable.

The cell phone, I must admit, can be of great use. But too often, it is used at the expense of others, even their safety. I don't want to be forced to hear about someone's personal life while waiting to see my doctor. I don't want to be forced to listen to someone's musical response to a phone call. I don't want to be worried about other drivers while they make an appointment for a manicure. A cell phone does not give people the right to ignore the rights and safety of others.

Voice mail has also changed a lot in recent years. How I wish I could call the gas company or electric company and immediately connect with the person to whom I need to speak. Now I have to press a series of numbers and listen to all kinds of electronic voices before I can even get close to my destination.

When television first came out, it was a novelty. For a while, it didn't affect my daily life very much, but as time went by, I became aware of how people were addicted to it. Today, my TV gets thousands of channels – most with almost as much advertising as programming – and I have to pay for it all! I have to pay to be told to buy things I either can't afford or don't want.

So, as our world becomes more and more controlled by our inventions, are we simplifying our lives, or complicating them?

Comments (9)

B For each pair of sentences, check (✓) the one the author would agree with.

1. ☐ a. The Internet provides reliable information all the time.

   ☐ b. The Internet is full of misinformation and opinions.

2. ☐ a. Cell phones can cause people to do dangerous things.

   ☐ b. Cell phones are the best invention since TV.

3. ☐ a. People's lives are negatively affected by TV.

   ☐ b. People's lives are not affected by TV.

4. ☐ a. Our inventions are controlling the world.

   ☐ b. Our inventions are simplifying the world.

4 Superstitions and beliefs

LESSON A · Superstitions

1

vocabulary

Match the phrases to make logical sentences.

1. I got into the best dorm on campus due to the ___e___
2. Muriel's never bowled, so her high score was ____
3. I tried to get tickets to the play, but I couldn't. I was ____
4. When Max graduated from college, I wished him the ____
5. Celia drives too fast. One day she's going to have an accident. I wish she wouldn't ____
6. I was hoping to find a letter in my mailbox, but ____
7. Jim dropped his laptop and lost his files. He's had some ____

a. push her luck.
b. bad luck.
c. best of luck.
d. out of luck.
e. luck of the draw.
f. beginner's luck.
g. no such luck.

2

grammar

Underline the reporting clauses in this paragraph.

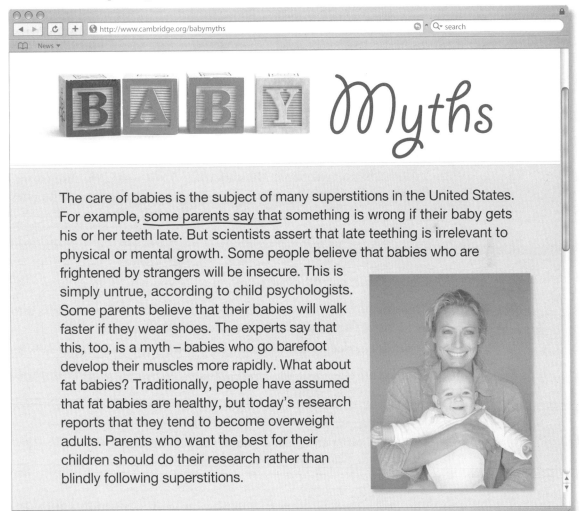

http://www.cambridge.org/babymyths

News ▼

BABY Myths

The care of babies is the subject of many superstitions in the United States. For example, <u>some parents say that</u> something is wrong if their baby gets his or her teeth late. But scientists assert that late teething is irrelevant to physical or mental growth. Some people believe that babies who are frightened by strangers will be insecure. This is simply untrue, according to child psychologists. Some parents believe that their babies will walk faster if they wear shoes. The experts say that this, too, is a myth – babies who go barefoot develop their muscles more rapidly. What about fat babies? Traditionally, people have assumed that fat babies are healthy, but today's research reports that they tend to become overweight adults. Parents who want the best for their children should do their research rather than blindly following superstitions.

3

grammar

Combine each pair of sentences using the words in parentheses.

1. As a child, I believed some strange things. A monster was living under my bed. (believe)

   As a child, I ___believed (that)___ a monster ___was living under my bed.___

2. To keep the monster away, I had to do certain things. I had to adjust the covers over me. (feel)

   To keep the monster away, I _____
   I _____

3. I needed extra protection. My stuffed bear would help me. (assume)

   I _____ my stuffed bear
   _____

4. I was fairly sure of one thing. My parents wouldn't believe me. (doubt)

   I _____
   my parents _____

4

grammar

Use the verbs in parentheses to explain what you would do in these situations.

1. Your friend won't travel on Friday the 13th because he considers it to be an unlucky day. How would you reassure him? (explain)

   I would explain that Friday the 13th is just like any other day.

2. Your soccer teammate saw you rubbing a charm for good luck. How would you explain this? (admit)

   _____

3. You aren't superstitious, but your friend claims that following some superstitions brings good luck. How would you respond? (argue)

   _____

4. You read an article about how the names given to Chinese babies are often chosen to be lucky. How would you tell someone about this article? (report)

   _____

A Read the text and answer the questions. Write the letter of the appropriate sentence.

writing

1. Which sentence is the thesis statement? _____

2. Which sentence gives general examples? _____

3. Which sentence reflects the author's personal opinion about traditional beliefs? _____

4. Which sentence restates the thesis statement? _____

Traditional Beliefs

a Traditional beliefs are not the same as superstitions. They differ in that they supposedly transmit useful information from one generation to another. **b** For example, I'm sure most of us can remember our parents telling us to eat certain foods or to avoid specific behaviors. Is there wisdom in these teachings, or are they without value? **c** Some of the beliefs passed down through the generations reflect current medical thinking, whereas others have not passed the test of time.

Carrots are good for your eyes!

Did your mother ever tell you to eat your carrots because they are good for your eyes? Scientists now report that eating carrots can help prevent a severe eye disease called macular degeneration. Because carrots are rich in a substance called beta carotene, eating just one carrot a day can reduce the likelihood of contracting this disease by 40 percent. Is garlic really good for you? It turns out that it is. It can kill the type of virus that causes colds. How about chicken soup? We now understand that chicken contains an amino acid that is similar to a drug often prescribed for people with respiratory infections.

Unfortunately, not all of Mom's advice has withstood medical inquiry. For example, generations of children have been told not to go swimming for an hour after eating. But research suggests that there is no danger in having lunch and then diving back into the ocean. Is chocolate really so bad for teenagers' skin? Doctors now believe that there is little connection between diet and an outbreak of acne. Does candy cause tooth decay? Well, yes and no. Sticky candy or other sweets made with grains tend to cause more decay than sweets made with simple sugars, which dissolve quickly in the mouth.

d Even though science can persuade us that some of our traditional beliefs don't hold water, there is still a lot of wisdom in the beliefs that have been handed down from generation to generation. **e** After all, much of this lore has been accumulated from thousands of years of trial-and-error experience in family health care. **f** We should respect this informal body of knowledge even as we search for clear scientific evidence to prove it true or false.

B Write a composition about traditional beliefs in your own culture. Tell about some you think are true, and some you think are not.

grammar

Read the article and underline the reporting verbs that are in the passive voice.

FAMOUS HOAXES

On October 30, 1938, perhaps the most famous broadcast in the entire history of radio took place. Heard all over the United States, the broadcast reported that a spacecraft from Mars had landed in a small town in New Jersey. It was said that the Martians were attacking the surrounding area with a "death ray." Radio reporters also claimed that three huge war machines had emerged from the spacecraft. After much destruction, it was reported that the Martians were dying. Specialists suggested that the Martians had no resistance to earth's infectious diseases.

Of course, this story was just a radio play, written and produced by a famous actor, Orson Welles, but many people believed it. It was reported that there was widespread panic throughout the country, especially in New Jersey. It has been suggested that Welles's broadcast offers many lessons about how the mass media can affect people.

Orson Welles

vocabulary

Cross out the word that does not fit the meaning of the sentence.

1. It is *conceivable* / *misleading* / *plausible* that many lowland areas will be under water if the current trend in climate change continues.

2. Fad diets that promise you'll lose 10 pounds the first day sound *convincing* / *fishy* / *far-fetched* to me. There's no way you can lose 10 pounds in one day!

3. Beware of *dubious* / *phony* / *well-founded* e-mails that ask you to supply personal information like your credit card number or your salary.

4. Greta gave such a *believable* / *convincing* / *iffy* performance in the play that I almost forgot she was acting!

5. Stephanie's blog is *misleading* / *fishy* / *believable*. Her profile says she's 24, but I know for a fact she's only 18.

6. That Carlos is a chef seems *far-fetched* / *dubious* / *conceivable* to me. The food he cooked for dinner was awful.

7. I don't believe life is possible on other planets. Show me a *plausible* / *dubious* / *well-founded* article that proves it, and then maybe I'll believe it.

8. When Kay told me she bought a car on the Internet, it sounded *iffy* / *far-fetched* / *credible* to me. But the car is actually pretty nice!

3

grammar

Use the words in parentheses to rewrite these sentences with a reporting clause in the passive with *it*.

1. Over one billion people use the Internet. (estimate)

   It's estimated (that) over one billion people use the Internet.

2. Every continent on earth has a city named Rome. (report)

   _____

3. The longest word in English without a vowel is "rhythm." (say)

   _____

4. In a baby's first year of life, parents lose between 400 and 750 hours of sleep. (believe)

   _____

5. Items like plastic cups and toys take 500 years to break down. (believe)

   _____

6. About 100 hairs fall from a person's head each day. (claim)

   _____

4

grammar

Use the cues to write a reporting clause in the passive.

1. suggest / traditional treatments such as acupuncture / are effective

   It is suggested (that) traditional treatments such as acupuncture are effective.

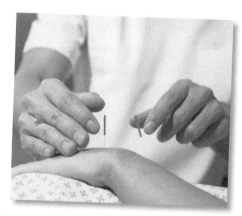

2. believe / average American child / watches 20,000 commercials each year

   _____

   _____

3. say / one hour of vigorous exercise / extends your life by two hours

   _____

   _____

4. claim / cure for cancer / will be found in ten years

   _____

   _____

5. report / animals / can predict earthquakes

   _____

   _____

5

reading

A Read the article about the possible extrasensory perception of dogs. Match the abilities on the left with the explanations on the right.

1. finding its way home _____
2. predicting thunderstorms _____
3. knowing if a buried person is alive or not _____

a. changes in barometric pressure
b. changes in the earth's magnetic field
c. infrared heat sensors on the dog's snout

The Amazing Abilities of DOGS

Do dogs have a sixth sense? Yes, but perhaps not in the way that is generally assumed. There is nothing supernatural about canine sensitivities. They can all be explained by biological mechanisms, although it is true that we are only beginning to understand some of them.

For instance, dogs can find their way home from long distances. It has been said that this ability is based on the detection of subtle differences and changes in the earth's magnetic field. We are still learning how dogs achieve such remarkable navigational feats as have been objectively recorded time and again.

Dogs are also capable of predicting thunderstorms. When a storm is imminent, they may become intensely alarmed and begin whimpering and trembling as if in pain. Their distress increases when the thunder starts to boom, but it can be observed for some time before the storm actually breaks overhead. This sensitivity is a response to changes in barometric pressure. It may seem to be meaningless behavior today, but in the dog's wild ancestry, it made good sense to become worried by these climactic signals. For example, wolves go to a great deal of trouble to build their dens on slopes, perhaps to protect tiny pups from floods. It is possible that domestic dogs are acting out the behavior of their ancestors' response to the danger of flooding.

One of the most amazing claims for the dog's sixth sense was made recently by researchers who reported that they had discovered infrared detectors in the dog's nose. This could explain certain abilities previously thought to be supernatural. St. Bernard dogs, for example, are said to be able to tell whether a climber buried in an avalanche is still alive, simply by sniffing the snow. If there are sensitive heat detectors in the noses of animals, this theory is not so far-fetched. We know that they exist on the snouts of certain snakes, and this strengthens the case for their existence in dogs.

B Check the statements that the author would probably agree with.

☐ 1. Dogs have more kinds of sensory perceptions than people.

☐ 2. Scientists will probably be able to discover how dogs' senses work.

☐ 3. The behavior of wolves is irrelevant to the understanding of dogs.

☐ 4. The behavior of some dogs during thunderstorms indicates that they are afraid of drowning.

☐ 5. The presence of heat detectors in some snakes proves that dogs have similar sensors.

5 Television and reading

1 grammar

Complete the e-mail with *so, such, so many, so few, so much,* or *so little.*

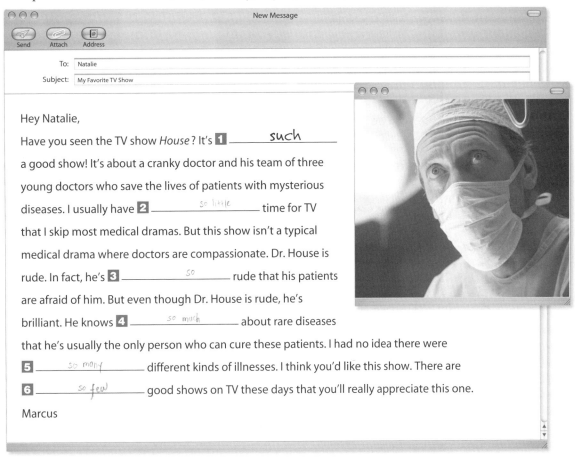

New Message

Send Attach Address

To: Natalie

Subject: My Favorite TV Show

Hey Natalie,

Have you seen the TV show *House*? It's **1** ___such___ a good show! It's about a cranky doctor and his team of three young doctors who save the lives of patients with mysterious diseases. I usually have **2** ___so little___ time for TV that I skip most medical dramas. But this show isn't a typical medical drama where doctors are compassionate. Dr. House is rude. In fact, he's **3** ___so___ rude that his patients are afraid of him. But even though Dr. House is rude, he's brilliant. He knows **4** ___so much___ about rare diseases that he's usually the only person who can cure these patients. I had no idea there were **5** ___so many___ different kinds of illnesses. I think you'd like this show. There are **6** ___so few___ good shows on TV these days that you'll really appreciate this one.

Marcus

2 vocabulary

Write the type of TV show next to its description.

cartoon ⁊	game show	reality TV ₉	soap opera ₂	talk show ₅
documentary ₆	news program ₃	sitcom ₈	sports program ₄	

___game show___ 1. Participants compete for money and prizes by answering questions that an average fifth grade student would know.

_____ 2. The complicated lives of the Diaz family are dramatized daily.

_____ 3. Ann Brady reports on the top news stories of the day.

_____ 4. The Lakers take on the Suns in game three of the playoffs.

_____ 5. Ty Ott interviews the actor Ash Lake and the chef Ami Tran.

_____ 6. Astronaut Neil Armstrong's life is reviewed in this program.

_____ 7. A boy and his ladybug friend star in this animated kids' show.

_____ 8. Alice Lee stars in this funny half-hour show about high school.

_____ 9. To win, chefs live together and cook dishes for celebrity judges.

3

grammar

Write six logical sentences by choosing one word or phrase from each column.

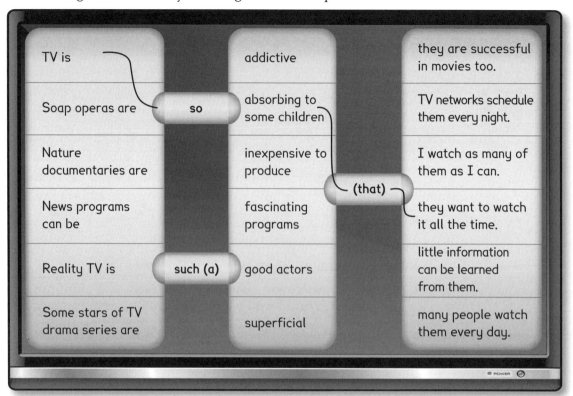

TV is	addictive	they are successful in movies too.
Soap operas are	**so**	absorbing to some children	TV networks schedule them every night.
Nature documentaries are	inexpensive to produce	I watch as many of them as I can.
News programs can be	fascinating programs	**(that)**	they want to watch it all the time.
Reality TV is	**such (a)**	good actors	little information can be learned from them.
Some stars of TV drama series are	superficial	many people watch them every day.

1. _TV is so absorbing to some children (that) they want to watch it all the time._

2. _____

3. _____

4. _____

5. _____

6. _____

4

grammar

Complete these sentences with opinions of your own.

1. Some drama series can be so _____violent_____ that _I don't think children_
   _should watch them._____

2. There are so many _____ TV shows to watch this season that I
   _____

3. _____ is such a great actor that I _____
   _____

4. _____ are such good nights to watch TV that _____
   _____

5. There are so few really funny shows on TV that I _____
   _____

6. Commercials can be so _____ that I _____
   _____

A Choose either a reality TV show or a drama series that you are familiar with, and write a review of it. Your review should answer the following questions.

writing

Reality TV show

1. What is the title of the reality show, and when is it on?

2. What kind of reality show is it, and where does it take place?

3. Are the cast members on this program likeable or not?

4. What kinds of challenges do the cast members participate in?

5. Would you want to participate in this reality show if you had the chance?

6. Would you recommend it to others? Why or why not?

The Amazing Race

Drama series

1. What is the title of the drama series, and when is it on?

2. What kind of drama series is it, and where does it take place?

3. Are the story lines believable or not?

4. Are the actors on this program good in their roles or not?

5. Is it original, or does it remind you of other shows you have seen?

6. Would you recommend it to others? Why or why not?

CSI: Crime Scene Investigation

_____

_____

_____

_____

_____

_____

_____

_____

_____

B Reread your review. Are there places where adding more details would make your writing better? If so, go back and add them.

1

vocabulary

Circle the words that best complete the sentences.

1. The last book I read wasn't original. In fact, it seemed pretty *formulaic* / *touching* to me.

2. My teacher was disappointed with the short story I wrote. She said my work was unoriginal and *engrossing* / *insipid.*

3. The last *Harry Potter* book was so *predictable* / *riveting* I read it in two days!

4. The way Nicholas Sparks describes the heartbreaking relationship between the two main characters in *The Notebook* is beautiful and *predictable* / *touching.*

5. I always worry when I read a Patricia Cornwell book. It's usually so *clichéd* / *engrossing* that I'd rather read the book than do my homework!

6. After I read the *inspiring* / *predictable* story of a woman who lost over 100 pounds, I followed her example and lost 20 pounds myself!

7. Cheap detective novels are usually *clichéd* / *moving,* but I love to read them anyway!

grammar

Underline the sentence adverbs in these dialogues. Then write them in the chart below.

1.   Jack: I don't trust the facts in this biography of Madonna.

         Lisa: Well, the author <u>clearly</u> did his research. Also, didn't he interview her extensively?

2.   Jill: When is your book going to be published?

         Fei: Apparently in May, but copies will be available to me in April.

3.   Aaron: I went to buy that new self-help book, but I couldn't find it.

    Emma: Haven't you heard? It was removed from the bookstores. Supposedly, the author used materials from other books without giving credit to the original authors.

4.   Kurt: I'm surprised. That new biography about John Lennon was so dull!

   Teresa: I know. The writer probably didn't even like The Beatles.

5.   Josh: This is the third murder mystery I've read this month.

     Tara: Obviously, you like that kind of book!

6. Kazuko: Robert Frost's poems seem to be about simple things.

     Julie: Yes, but unquestionably, a more careful reading reveals deeper meaning.

Certainty	Less certainty	Possibility
clearly		

3

grammar

Rewrite these sentences using the sentence adverbs in parentheses.

1. Reading nonfiction is more educational than reading novels. (apparently)
   <u>Reading nonfiction is apparently more educational than reading novels.</u>
   <u>Apparently, reading nonfiction is more educational than reading novels.</u>

2. Young people today are not interested in reading newspapers. (frankly)
   _____

3. There is a magazine for almost any interest that a person might have. (definitely)
   _____

4. Young adults would read more if they had access to technology like online libraries and e-books. (probably)
   _____

5. Because of the Internet, newspapers and magazines will disappear in the future. (potentially)
   _____

4

grammar

How does reading books and magazines compare with reading material on the Internet? Write sentences using sentence adverbs.

1. <u>Reading a book in bed</u> is clearly <u>more comfortable than reading</u>
   <u>a book online.</u>

2. _____ is potentially _____
   _____

3. Apparently, _____
   _____

4. _____ unquestionably the most _____
   _____

5. Supposedly, _____
   _____

6. Unfortunately, _____

reading

A Read the book reviews below to find the answers to these questions. Then read the book reviews again carefully.

1. How long did it take the reviewer to read *Marley & Me*? _____

2. What language are the foreign words from in *The Kite Runner*? _____

Marley & Me: Life and Love with the World's Worst Dog
by John Grogan

I just finished *Marley & Me* last night. I had picked it up last weekend at the bookstore because the adorable photo on the cover caught my eye. Being an avid animal and dog lover, I couldn't pass it up.

Needless to say, I devoured the book in two days. To me it was refreshing to see such commitment in another dog owner. I have always believed that when you adopt a pet it is a lifelong commitment. Grogan articulates this idea without becoming overly emotional.

Grogan's writing is unquestionably clear, interesting, and down-to-earth. I couldn't put the book down. It is a joy to read, as well as a touching story. When you close it in the end, your heart will feel like it is too large to fit inside your chest.

The Kite Runner
by Khaled Hosseini

The Kite Runner is a beautiful novel by Afghan-American Khaled Hosseini that ranks among the best stories of this century.

Hosseini's first novel tells a heartbreaking story of the unlikely friendship between Amir, the son of a wealthy Afghan businessman, and Hassan, the son of the businessman's servant.

One is born to a father of enormous authority, the other to a crippled man. Amir and Hassan live and play together, not simply as friends, but as brothers without mothers. Loyalty and blood are the ties that bind their stories into a moving and unexpected plot. Even though exotic Afghan customs and Farsi words pop up occasionally, they are so well defined for the reader that the book is enlightening, not at all tedious.

Hosseini is an original and gifted writer. His canvas might be a place and time we barely understand, but in *The Kite Runner* he paints his art on the page, where it is personal and touching to us all.

B Check (✓) whether each statement applies to *Marley & Me*, *The Kite Runner*, or both.

	Marley & Me	The Kite Runner	Both
1. Two boys share a close relationship.	☐	☐	☐
2. The story is deeply touching and moving.	☐	☐	☐
3. Having a pet is a big responsibility.	☐	☐	☐
4. A dog makes an impression on a man's life.	☐	☐	☐
5. The two main characters do not have mothers.	☐	☐	☐
6. The writing is extremely understandable.	☐	☐	☐

6 Musicians and music

1

grammar

Circle the words that best complete the sentences.

1. Generally, the more a singer is known, the (more)/ less money he or she makes.

2. The less publicity a musician gets, the *easier / harder* it is to make a living.

3. Some say the earlier you expose children to classical music, the *more / less* likely they are to excel in school.

4. The more relaxing the music, the *faster / slower* I fall asleep.

5. In my opinion, the more you learn about some musicians, the *fewer / less* you are able to understand them.

6. For many music fans, the more difficult it is to find a song or album, the *better / sooner*!

2

grammar

Complete Lily's interview with the words from the box.

better	less	longer	more	sooner

Lily: When did you realize you wanted to be a guitarist?

Shane: I was ten years old. My brother was taking guitar lessons and the more I heard him practice, the (1) _____more_____ I knew I could play better.

Lily: Who were your biggest musical influences?

Shane: My biggest influence was Prince. The more I listened to his music, the (2) _____ it got.

Lily: Prince is great, but your music doesn't sound like his.

Shane: Yeah, I know. I realized the more I listened to Prince's music, the (3) _____ I wanted to sound like him. I wanted my own sound – something that made me unique.

Lily: You've certainly succeeded! What's next for you?

Shane: I'm moving to New York City. The (4) _____ I stay in Los Angeles, the more I realize I need a change.

Lily: Why is that?

Shane: The music scene in New York is awesome.

Lily: When will you leave?

Shane: I'm not sure yet, but I think the (5) _____ I leave, the better.

vocabulary

Choose the adjective that best describes your opinion of each kind of music. Then write a sentence explaining why.

1. pop (catchy / frenetic / monotonous)
   I love catchy pop songs. I can't get Christina
   Aguilera's new song out of my head!

2. classical (exhilarating / haunting / soothing)
   _____
   _____

3. jazz (evocative / soothing / frenetic)
   _____
   _____

4. hip-hop (catchy / evocative / monotonous)
   _____
   _____

5. folk (haunting / soothing / catchy)
   _____

6. rock (monotonous / exhilarating / frenetic)
   _____

Christina Aguilera

grammar

Rewrite these sentences to make them true for you. If the sentence is already true for you, write a sentence to support your opinion.

1. The more I listen to opera, the more I like it.
   The more I listen to opera, the less I like it.

2. The more unusual a musician is, the less I like his or her music.
   _____

3. The more musicians put political opinions in songs, the less I enjoy them.
   _____

4. The more kinds of music there are online, the fewer opportunities we'll have to learn about different cultures.
   _____

5. The more time teens spend listening to music, the less time they will spend learning about more important things.
   _____

6. The fewer independent radio stations, the less likely it will be to hear diverse music.
   _____

writing

A Read the characteristics of listening to live music and listening to recorded music. Then put them under the correct heading below.

You listen with many other people.	You can listen to a song over and over.
Sometimes you hear music you don't like.	You can listen to any kind of music you're in the mood for.
You can't see the musicians while you listen.	
You can sing along with your favorite songs.	You can listen to music in any order you'd like.
You can adjust the volume.	You can turn off or skip songs you don't like.
You can hear music by well-known artists.	You can listen only when musicians are playing
You can't adjust the volume.	on stage.

Live music

_____

_____

_____

_____

Recorded music

_____

_____

_____

_____

Live music and recorded music

_____

_____

_____

_____

B What is your opinion of listening to live music versus listening to recorded music? Write a thesis statement expressing your opinion on the subject.

_____

_____

_____

C Now write a compare-and-contrast essay. Include your thesis statement in the introduction, two paragraphs describing the similarities and differences, and a conclusion restating your point of view.

vocabulary

Correct the underlined mistake in each sentence with one of the words in the box. Some words will be used more than once.

be	break	get	make	pay

1. Most musicians must <u>break</u> their dues before they become successful. ___pay___
2. After retiring in 2000, my favorite band is planning to <u>get</u> a comeback. ___make___
3. Nelly Furtado's latest song is going to <u>pay</u> a big hit. ___be___
4. I want to be a singer. What advice do you have to <u>make</u> into the business? ___break___
5. Many singing stars <u>be</u> their big break as contestants on *American Idol*. ___get___
6. It was so difficult for Jay-Z to <u>break</u> his foot in the door that he started his own recording label. ___get___
7. The first time I heard Madonna, I knew she wouldn't <u>pay</u> a one-hit wonder. ___be___
8. While some musicians may be talented and work hard, they might never <u>get</u> a name for themselves in the music industry. ___make___

grammar

Complete these dialogues. Use the verbs in parentheses and *would* or *will*.

1. Kim: I used to listen to all kinds of music when I was younger.

    Ron: Not me! When I was young, I __would listen__ (listen) only to rock music.

2. Dan: You play the guitar so well. How often do you practice?

    Sally: I practice all the time. In fact, I ___will___ (practice) four to five hours a day depending on my schedule.

3. Mario: What do you do in your spare time?

    Kate: I don't have much spare time, but when I do, I ___will___ (surf) the Internet to learn where my favorite band is playing.

4. Kristen: I can't believe the lead singer of the band we saw spent so much time after the show talking with his fans and signing autographs.

    Amy: I know. Most singers these days ___won't / will not___ (not spend) any time with their fans, let alone sign an autograph!

5. Paula: When I was a teenager, I loved to listen to music that was really loud.

    Diana: Me, too. In fact, I ___would___ (turn up) my stereo as loud as I could.

6. Rob: I just heard a Beatles song from years ago.

    Lori: I love The Beatles! In college I ___would___ (listen) to them every day.

3

grammar

Read the sentences about a band. Then check (✓) the sentences that have mistakes and correct them.

☑ 1. When the band comes onstage, the crowd would scream.
   <u>When the band comes onstage, the crowd will scream.</u>

☐ 2. Before the band got popular, it will never play before a sellout crowd.
   _____

☐ 3. Years ago, only bands with great musicianship would usually make it big.
   _____

☐ 4. When the guitarist was young, he would practice in front of a mirror.
   _____

☐ 5. In the past, the band will play only hard rock songs.
   _____

☐ 6. Although the band used to give autographs after a show, these days security guards would not let fans backstage.
   _____

4

grammar

Which music habits were or were not true for you in the past? Which are or are not true for you now? Write sentences with *would* or *will*.

1. listen to a CD over and over again
   <u>When I find a CD I really love, I will listen to it over and over again.</u>

2. listen to very loud music
   _____

3. spend a lot of money on CDs and music downloads
   _____

4. enjoy playing an instrument
   _____

5. travel long distances to see live concerts of favorite bands
   _____

6. argue with family members about musical tastes
   _____

A Read the article. What do you think the root *neuro-* means?

Music May Someday Help Repair the Brain

The music that makes the foot tap, the fingers snap, and the pulse quicken stirs the brain at its most fundamental levels, suggesting that scientists one day may be able to retune damaged minds by exploiting rhythm, harmony, and melody, according to new research.

"Undeniably, there is a biology of music," said Harvard University Medical School neurobiologist Mark Jude Tramo. "Music is biologically part of human life, just as music is aesthetically part of human life."

RESEARCHERS FOUND THAT THE BRAIN:

■ Responds directly to harmony. Neuroscientists discovered that different parts of the brain involved in emotion are activated depending on whether the music is pleasant or unpleasant.

■ Interprets written music in an area on the brain's right side. That region corresponds to an area on the opposite side of the brain known to handle written words and letters. So, researchers uncovered an anatomical link between music and language.

■ Grows in response to musical training. In a study of classically trained musicians, researchers discovered that male musicians have significantly larger brains than men who have not had extensive musical training.

Overall, music seems to involve the brain at almost every level, and researchers are already looking for ways to harness the power of music to change the brain. Preliminary research also suggests that music may play some role in enhancing intelligence. Indeed, so seductive is the possibility that music can boost a child's IQ that some politicians are lobbying for school children to be exposed regularly to Mozart sonatas, although such research has yet to be confirmed.

The scientists said the new research could help the clinical practice of neurology, including cognitive rehabilitation. As a therapeutic tool, for example, some doctors already use music to help rehabilitate stroke patients. Surprisingly, some stroke patients who have lost their ability to speak retain their ability to sing, and that opens an avenue for therapists to retrain the brain's speech centers.

B Read the statements. Are they supported by research? Check (✔) yes or no.

	Yes	No
1. Different areas of the brain respond to music.	☐	☐
2. The brains of classically trained male musicians grow larger than the brains of nonmusical males.	☐	☐
3. The brains of classically trained female musicians do not grow larger than nonmusical females.	☐	☐
4. Children who listen to Mozart sonatas develop higher intelligence than those who do not have exposure to this music.	☐	☐
5. Some stroke victims who are unable to speak are able to sing.	☐	☐

Changing times

grammar

Underline the relative pronouns in this announcement.

If these statements describe your situation, then telecommuting may be right for you.

1. You have a job <u>that</u> you can do independently of your co-workers.

2. You can work productively without the pressure <u>that</u> you may get from supervisors.

3. Your home has a quiet room, <u>which</u> you can use as your office.

4. You have the office equipment <u>that</u> you will need to do your job at home.

5. There are no family members <u>who</u> will bother you while you are trying to work.

6. You won't miss the social interaction <u>that</u> many people enjoy in the workplace.

7. You don't get distracted by household chores, <u>which</u> interfere with your work.

8. You can effectively use the telephone and e-mail to communicate with your co-workers, <u>whose</u> help you may need while you are away from the office.

See your Human Resources representative for details of our telecommuting policy.

grammar

Combine these sentences using a relative pronoun. Then write O if the relative pronoun is optional and R if the relative pronoun is required.

___O___ 1. Physical fitness is an important goal. A lot of people try to achieve this goal.

Physical fitness is an important goal that a lot of people try to achieve.

___R___ 2. Many people stay fit. These people find the time to work out regularly at a gym.

_____

___O___ 3. For the best results, it's important to find a gym. You like this gym. *that*

_____

___R___ 4. It may be a good idea to hire a trainer. A trainer can work with you privately. *who*

_____

___R___ 5. Your trainer can give you advice. The advice can help you avoid injuries. *that which*

_____

___O___ 6. If you get bored at the gym, try bringing an MP3 player. You can listen to this MP3 player while you exercise. *that*

_____

3

vocabulary

Complete these conversations with words from the box.

| consistent | inconsiderate | indecisive | immature | logical | responsible |

1. A: Jim is 40 years old and watches cartoons.

   B: I know. He really is ____immature____ .

2. A: I can't make up my mind. Which tie looks better?

   B: Don't be so ____indecisive____ . Just choose one.

3. A: Why did Meredith buy such a large car with gas prices so high?

   B: I know it doesn't seem ____logical____ , but she needed a big car for her catering business.

4. A: Doesn't Allison look great? What is she doing to lose weight?

   B: She's been eating healthy and exercising on a ____consistent____ basis.

5. B: I don't like how e-mail is changing the way people communicate.

   A: I know. ____inconsiderate____ e-mails can really hurt someone's feelings.

6. A: I really like the new waiter you hired. He's very polite and dependable.

   B: Yes, he is. Even though he's young, he's quite ____responsible____ .

4

grammar

Use relative clauses and information of your own to complete these sentences.

1. I have always admired people __who are good at organizing their time.__

2. I've always thought that I would enjoy a lifestyle _____

   _____

3. Mothers _____

   _____ should be greatly admired.

4. These days many people want jobs _____

   _____

5. Finding enough time to spend with family and friends is a problem _____

   _____

writing

A Read this composition and answer the questions.

The family that eats together, stays together

I feel it is very important for families to have regular meals together. One of my most positive childhood memories was dinner with my parents and two sisters. As a result, last year I decided that the entire family would have dinner together three days a week. Because my husband and I both work and our three kids are busy with school activities, we found that we rarely had a chance to get together as a family. But we thought it would be possible for everyone to set aside three evenings a week for a sit-down dinner.

First we tried setting three fixed days for our experiment – Mondays, Wednesdays, and Fridays. After a couple of weeks of trying this plan, almost everyone was unhappy. Then my son had the idea of having everyone post his or her schedule for the week on the refrigerator every Sunday. I would choose the three best days, and those with scheduling conflicts. . . .

For a while, the kids continued to resist the idea. They said they would rather spend the time with their friends or participating in sports or other activities. Gradually, though, they began to see these evenings together in a very positive way. We laughed a lot. We made vacation plans. We discussed each other's problems. After a couple of months, anyone who had to miss a family meal felt. . . .

We all feel that we have been able to build much stronger relationships within the family than we had before. Of course, there are still disagreements, but we communicate better with each other now. The idea of having regular family meals together, which seemed difficult at first, has brought about many positive changes in our lives.

1. What is the thesis statement?

   _____

2. What is the focus of the second paragraph?

   _____

3. What is the focus of the third paragraph?

   _____

4. What sentence in the conclusion restates the thesis statement?

   _____

B Write a thesis statement for a composition about an important decision you have made recently.

   _____

   _____

C Now write your composition. Include two paragraphs providing background information and details, and a conclusion.

grammar

Circle the expressions that best complete the sentences.

1. (Like)/ *As though* my mother before me, I serve a traditional dinner on special holidays for my family to enjoy.

2. Doesn't it seem *the way / as if* good manners are a thing of the past?

3. Elena feels *as / as though* the stories her grandfather told her as a child will be forgotten unless she shares them with her friends and family.

4. Craftsmen today still make Moravian tiles *as / as if* they were made in the early 20th century.

5. Schools should offer music and art *as if / the way* they did when I was a student.

6. *As / As though* my aunt always says, "Make new friends, but keep your old ones."

7. Some days I feel *as if / the way* time passes too quickly.

8. Modern kabuki performers wear elaborate makeup and costumes *like / as though* their Japanese ancestors did centuries ago.

vocabulary

Choose the expressions that exemplify each situation.

a. advocate change	c. block a change e. cope with change
b. facilitate a change	d. resist change f. welcome a change

___c___ 1. Students worked together to overturn the school's recent decision to make students wear uniforms.

___b___ 2. Mr. Viera helped our office switch from using an outdated e-mail program to a newer, more efficient e-mail program.

___f___ 3. After being on a plane for eight hours, Joe was happy to finally land in Hawaii and begin his vacation.

___d___ 4. Eun Ju orders the same dish every time she goes out to eat. She refuses to try anything else on the menu.

___e___ 5. When Mark first retired from his job, he had trouble finding ways to fill his time. Now he plays golf and volunteers at the food bank.

___a___ 6. The politician gave an inspiring speech about supporting alternative energy sources. He said incorporating small changes in our lives will have huge benefits for the environment.

3

grammar

Read each situation and answer the questions using *as if*, *as though*, or *like*.

1. Cal used to look forward to going fishing with his son every summer. Now, his son doesn't want to go anymore. How does Cal feel?

   <u>He feels as if he has lost a</u>

   <u>family tradition.</u>

2. Anna loves origami, the Japanese art of paper folding. She wants to teach her daughter, but she doesn't want to learn. How does Anna feel?

   _____

   _____

3. Mia used to spend a lot of time with her grandmother. Since Mia moved away, she doesn't see her grandmother anymore. How does Mia feel?

   _____

   _____

4. Chris was playing ball in the house and broke a vase that has been in his mother's family for over 80 years. How does Chris feel?

   _____

   _____

4

grammar

Complete these sentences so that they are true for you.

1. I feel <u>as though my family traditions</u> aren't as strong as they used to be.

2. I don't feel _____
   _____ the way I did when I was younger.

3. These days I think many people act as if _____
   _____

4. I still _____
   _____ my family did years ago.

5. I feel _____
   _____ before too much time passes.

reading

A Read the article. Find the words and phrases in boldface that match the definitions.

1. a 100-year-old person <u>centenarian</u>
2. remove or reduce _____
3. mentally very healthy _____
4. an advanced number of years _____

Centenerian Planning

If you thought retirement planning is hard, wait until you get a glimpse of "**centenarian** planning." You'd better pull up a rocking chair.

It has been predicted that millions of people currently 50 and older will make it to the age of 100, says neuropsychologist Margery H. Silver, associate director of the New England Centenarian Study. "It is predicted that every female child born today has a 50-50 chance of living to be 100," she says.

An instructor in psychology at Harvard Medical School, Silver says one conclusion to emerge from the study of centenarians in the Boston area is that if you are going to live to be 100, you have to plan to live a healthy and forward-looking lifestyle. Not only will that help you reach a **ripe old age**, it will make living to 100 more worthwhile if you do. One of Silver's findings in the study is that a quarter of its centenarians were "cognitively intact," and

another substantial number were "thinking quite well," she says.

The lesson from those who were **sharp as a tack** at age 100? "Keep mentally active," says Silver, recounting how one of her centenarians, at 104, learned an entirely new branch of mathematics and started writing articles about it. "Exercising your brain is as important as exercising your body," she says. As for physical well-being, Silver feels as if some people have the genetic edge in reaching 100 – but lifestyle choices count for a lot. "Most of us have the genetic factor to live into our eighties," says Silver, "so we really need to pay attention to taking good care of our health." Also, making preventive health choices in our lives early on – such as avoiding saturated fats, keeping slim, avoiding too much sun, exercising, and taking the right vitamins – can add 10 or more quality years to anyone's life, explains Silver. Of course, not doing those things can **subtract** years.

B Check the advice that the article mentions.

☐ 1. Avoid habits that lead to bad health, such as eating saturated fats.

☐ 2. Do things to keep your mind active.

☐ 3. Get lots of sun as often as possible.

☐ 4. Practice physical fitness.

☐ 5. Get an annual checkup from your doctor.

☐ 6. Avoid vitamins.

8 Consumer culture

LESSON A · What's new on the market?

1
grammar

Underline the direct objects and circle the indirect objects in each sentence.

1. Some stores offer (their customers) frequent-buyer cards as incentives to come back and buy more.
2. Advertising is useful because it tells us news about improved products.
3. The salesperson recommended the plasma-screen TV to me.
4. Someone had to explain the new printer to Daniel.
5. This GPS system must have cost you a lot of money.
6. You should mail this card to the company for a rebate.
7. Online auction sites offer shoppers great ways to save money.
8. I don't shop online because I like to ask salespeople questions in person.

2
grammar

Unscramble the words and phrases to make correct sentences.

1. the latest laptops / showed / the woman / the salesperson
   The salesperson showed the woman the latest laptops.

2. the woman / to / the IXL-6000 / recommended / the salesperson
   _____
   _____

3. her / the main features / he / described / to
   _____

4. him / the woman / the price / asked
   _____

5. the salesperson / $2,100 / her / told
   _____

6. said nothing / to / him / she / for a moment
   _____

7. a discount / offered / the salesperson / her
   _____

8. the money / the salesperson / she / to / gave
   _____

grammar

Use the words in the box to give advice about what to do in each situation.

lend	mention	recommend	return	teach

1. Mai got a jazz music CD from her brother for her birthday, but she prefers pop.
   <u>Mai should return the jazz music CD to the store.</u>

2. Ian and Pam want to go skiing with Kate, but Pam doesn't have enough money.
   _____

3. Ty is a computer specialist. His sister wants a computer, but she doesn't
   know much about them.
   _____

4. Jessica's favorite Italian restaurant is Luigi's. Her father wants to eat Italian
   food but doesn't know any restaurants.
   _____

5. Max sold his car to a neighbor. The car uses a lot of oil, but he forgot to say
   anything about it. His neighbor is going to take a long trip.
   _____

vocabulary

Write a sentence about each situation using the expressions in the box.

bargain hunter	compulsive shopper	shopping spree
buyer's remorse	credit limit	window-shopping

1. Monica and Emil love to see what's on sale at their favorite stores. They
   can spend hours doing this, without buying anything at all!
   <u>Both Monica and Emil love to go window-shopping.</u>

2. When Gerry gets paid, he always buys things for himself, whether he needs
   them or not. He often spends all of his money in one day.
   _____

3. Mark never pays full price for anything. He always searches for the best
   price. He even goes to different parts of town to get a good price.
   _____

4. Before her wedding, Anne and her mother went shopping for everything they
   would need for the wedding. They spent a lot of money and had a great time.
   _____

5. Jan bought an expensive pair of earrings today. She loved them at the store,
   but now that she's home, she feels guilty for spending so much money.
   _____

6. While Eric was on vacation, he used his credit card for everything. At the
   end of the trip, he tried to buy a present but his card was denied.
   _____

5

writing

A For each opinion, check (✓) the two supporting examples or details that support it. Then write another sentence to support the opinion.

1. Today's children are too materialistic.

☐ a. Many children have more free time than they have ever had before.

☐ b. They compete to have the coolest clothes and the most expensive hobbies.

☐ c. Parents complain that children only want money from them.

_____

_____

2. Digital cameras are superior to traditional cameras.

☐ a. Digital cameras don't require film, so in the long run they are cheaper.

☐ b. A good traditional camera costs about the same as a good digital camera.

☐ c. Pictures are a good keepsake.

_____

_____

3. Using an online supermarket saves you time and money.

☐ a. Groceries purchased online are delivered directly to your home.

☐ b. There's less chance to make an impulse buy because you're not actually in the store.

☐ c. It's easier to find rare or exotic foods while using an online supermarket.

_____

_____

B Write a thesis statement about one of the opinions above or one of your own.

_____

_____

C Write a composition. Include your thesis statement in the first paragraph, and develop your opinion with examples and details in subsequent paragraphs.

LESSON B · Consumer awareness

grammar

Read the letter from a customer to the owner of a supermarket. Underline the subjunctive verbs.

> Dear Ms. Munson:
>
> I saw the sales flier for Munson's Market, and I felt it was imperative that I <u>write</u> you. All the food on sale this week is snack food or highly processed food. Although I buy these foods occasionally, I suggest that healthy food be on sale too. It's crucial that people have the chance to buy affordable healthy foods, and I recommend that your supermarket start putting them on sale. I also propose that you offer a larger selection of fresh fruits and vegetables. Many people don't buy fresh foods because they just don't know about them. I think it's essential that your customers get the chance to incorporate these foods into their meals.
> Thank you.
>
> *Marcella Guzman*
> Marcella Guzman

grammar

Use the words in parentheses to rewrite each sentence using the subjunctive.

1. People should be on the lookout for false advertising. (it is important)
   <u>It is important that people be on the lookout for false advertising.</u>

2. Children should eat fast food only once or twice a month. (it is vital)
   _____

3. Parents should read reviews before their children see a movie. (it is crucial)
   _____

4. The government must prevent kids from dropping out of school. (we insist)
   _____

grammar

Complete these sentences with ideas of your own.

1. If you are suspicious about an ad for a product, I suggest that <u>you go to a</u>
   <u>comparison-shopping website and read about it.</u>

2. If you find an ad offensive, I recommend that _____
   _____

3. If you think a particular product is good, I propose that _____
   _____

4. If you want to pursue a career in advertising, it is important that _____
   _____

46 Unit 8 **Consumer culture**

vocabulary

What marketing strategies would you use for each product? Use the phrases in the box to write a sentence explaining your decision.

behavioral targeting	e-mail spam	frequent-buyer programs	product placement
celebrity endorsements	free samples	online TV commercials	telemarketing

1. ice cream I would use free samples because everyone would taste it and many people might like it so much they'd buy it.

2. investment services _____

3. a new restaurant _____

4. sports equipment _____

5. a health club _____

6. MP3 players _____

5 reading

A Read the article quickly. Check (✓) the behaviors of a shopaholic.

- ☐ overeating
- ☐ enjoying ceremonies
- ☐ buying more than necessary
- ☐ avoiding long-term problems
- ☐ feeling sad

Behavior Study of Shopaholics

Compulsive shoppers may have a new psychological excuse to blame for their wild shopping sprees. Psychologists at the University of Canterbury in New Zealand are investigating the "shop-till-you-drop" habit as a behavioral disorder comparable to binge eating. The symptoms are that shoppers frequently buy more than they can afford or more than they need, and it causes them distress. Compulsive shopping was first identified in 1915, but few studies have been done on the problem.

"It becomes a problem when you are out of control," senior psychology lecturer Neville Blampied said. "When you are feeling sad and blue, what do you do? Some people eat chocolate cake and half a quart of ice cream. Some people take the credit card and go out to the mall."

An advertisement in a local newspaper, calling for volunteers to participate in an experimental treatment program designed by Blampied, attracted only ten replies. But the problem, he said, is "clearly not rare." Compulsive eaters or shoppers get a kick from their habit. "Both activities provide an immediate kind of arousal and a bit of a boost," he said. "You have long-term problems in consequence, but human beings are extremely good at discounting long-term problems and are hypersensitive to short-term benefits."

The therapy's aim was to help people find better ways of managing their negative emotions. "You often have to start to get people to correctly recognize their emotions," Blampied said. "Not being able to discriminate what you really feel impairs your ability to solve the problem associated with what's making you feel that way."

B Check (✓) the correct answer for each question.

1. What is this article mostly about?
   - ☐ a. the warning signs of compulsive shopping
   - ☐ b. effective treatments for compulsive shopping
   - ☐ c. how compulsive shopping is a psychological problem

2. When might people indulge in compulsive shopping?
   - ☐ a. when they have lots of money
   - ☐ b. when they are feeling sad
   - ☐ c. when they participate in stress-management programs

3. Which is considered to be important in therapy for compulsive shoppers?
   - ☐ a. teaching them to manage their money better
   - ☐ b. teaching them to understand their emotions
   - ☐ c. encouraging them to give up their credit cards

9 Animals

LESSON A · Animals in our lives

1
grammar

Complete these sentences using *whenever* or *wherever*. If the time or place is specified, use *when* or *where*.

1. For some reason, _____ **wherever** _____ I go with my pet snake, someone gets upset.

2. Cats will sometimes leave dead mice on their owner's doorsteps _____ they want to show affection.

3. Research indicates that _____ a person strokes animals, his or her blood pressure goes down. Also, it's been argued that trained dogs should be present _____ there are people recovering from illnesses.

4. I recently visited a facility _____ dogs are trained to rescue victims from disasters such as earthquakes.

5. _____ I adopted my dog, I took on a serious responsibility. Being able to keep a pet healthy and happy depends on your lifestyle.

2
grammar

Rewrite the last sentence of each dialogue with a sentence including a clause starting with *whenever* or *wherever*.

1. A: I'm going over to Nancy's apartment. Would you like to come with me?
   B: No, I can't. She has a cat, and I'm allergic to them. Any time I'm around a cat, I start sneezing.
      _Whenever I'm around a cat, I start sneezing._____

2. A: Did you enjoy your walk in the park?
   B: Yes, but no matter where I went, dogs were running around without leashes.
      _____

3. A: What's wrong with your cat? She looks upset.
   B: She's just excited. She looks like that any time she sees a bird outside.
      _____

4. A: What kind of pet would you like to have?
   B: I love fish. Any time I watch fish swimming, I feel calm.
      _____

Write the correct word under each picture.

vocabulary

antennae	fangs	fin	hooves	paws	talons
beak	feathers	gills	horns	tail	wing

1. _____beak_____ 2. _____ 3. _____

4. _____ 5. _____ 6. _____

7. _____ 8. _____ 9. _____

10. _____ 11. _____ 12. _____

Combine the phrases from the two columns to make logical sentences.

grammar

Whenever I see a puppy,	there is sunlight and fresh air.
Pet reptiles should be kept where	they should have time to care for them.
Whenever people have pets,	I want to get one.
A caged bird cannot fly wherever	it chooses to go.

1. _____

2. _____

3. _____

4. _____

5

writing

A Read the thesis statements. Do the topics belong in the composition?
Check (✓) yes or no.

	Yes	No
1. Thesis statement: Owning a pet has many health benefits.		
a. People who own pets often have better physical health than people who do not own pets.	☐	☐
b. People who own pets handle daily stresses better.	☐	☐
c. Women who own pets care for their pets better than their own children.	☐	☐
d. People who have pets may be happier than other people.	☐	☐
2. Thesis statement: There are three types of exotic pets.		
a. Some pet birds, such as parrots and toucans, are exotic.	☐	☐
b. Reptiles like iguanas and snakes are considered exotic pets.	☐	☐
c. There are also mammals, such as ferrets and bats, that are exotic pets.	☐	☐
d. Exotic animals can transmit deadly diseases to their owners.	☐	☐
3. Thesis statement: Humans rely on animals for inspiration in the arts.		
a. Animals are often the main images in paintings, such as those of artist Henri Rousseau.	☐	☐
b. Author George Orwell used talking animals as the main characters in his political novel *Animal Farm*.	☐	☐
c. Movies such as *The Lion King* and *Ice Age* use animals to tell human stories of love and loyalty.	☐	☐
d. Animals bring great joy to humans.	☐	☐

B How would you choose to classify how animals are viewed in your culture?
Write a thesis statement and three topics.

Thesis statement: _____

_____

1. _____

_____

2. _____

_____

3. _____

_____

grammar

Complete the sentences with *whoever* or *whatever*.

1. ___Whoever___ can afford dog accessories like jeweled collars must have a lot of money!

2. _____ arguments I make about the benefits of owning a pet, my parents still won't let me have one.

3. When bringing a pet on a plane, you should be prepared to pay _____ the airline charges to transport it.

4. I wouldn't have a snake as a pet, but _____ does is very brave, in my opinion.

5. _____ has put a cat into a cat carrier knows it will try to get out.

6. _____ the weather, I always take my dog for a walk in the morning.

vocabulary

Use the expressions in the box to write a response to each question.

busy as a bee	quiet as a mouse	sly as a fox
gentle as a lamb	sick as a dog	strong as an ox

1. You are impressed that your brother can lift all the heavy boxes you packed while moving to a new apartment. What do you say?

   _My brother is as strong as an ox!_____

2. A friend asks you to the movies, but you're in bed with the flu. What do you say?

   _____

3. Your roommate comes home late, but she's careful not to wake you up. How do you describe her?

   _____

4. You ask your sister to lunch, but she has shopping to do, a deadline at work, and a doctor's appointment. How do you describe her?

   _____

5. You have been shopping for a car and a salesperson offers you a deal that sounds too good to be true. You don't trust him. How do you describe him?

   _____

6. You're afraid to pet your friend's dog. Your friend tells you that her dog is quiet and calm. What does your friend say?

   _____

3
grammar

Do you agree or disagree with these statements? Respond to what the first speaker says. Write sentences with *whoever* or *whatever*.

1. A: It's OK to pet a dog that you don't know well.

   B: <u>I disagree. Whoever pets a dog he or she</u>
   <u>doesn't know well might get bitten.</u>

2. A: Any dangerous animal, such as a wolf or a bear, should not be raised as a pet.

   B: _____
   _____

3. A: Anyone who finds a lost pet should demand a reward from its owner.

   B: _____
   _____

4. A: Any person who claims not to be afraid of a large barking dog is lying.

   B: _____
   _____

5. A: We should admire everybody who fights for the rights of animals.

   B: _____
   _____

4
grammar

Complete these sentences with ideas of your own. Use *whoever* or *whatever*.

1. <u>Whoever wants a playful, energetic pet</u> should think about getting a ferret.

2. Whatever information about pets you're looking for, _____
   _____

3. _____
   _____ must have plenty of space and a park nearby.

4. If I could have whatever pet I wanted, I would _____
   _____

5. _____
   _____ should not mind finding fur all over their clothes!

A Read the title and first paragraph of this story, and answer the questions. Then read the rest of the story.

reading

1. Do you think the people in the story will have good or bad luck?

   _____

2. Do you think that this will be a true story? _____

A Fairy Tale Comes True

Every Bosnian child knows the story of a poor woman who caught a golden fish, released it, and in return gained wealth and happiness. It's a Balkan fairy tale, but it turned into reality for one poor family. "Whatever happened here is beyond good luck – it really is a fable," said Admir Malkoc.

In 1990, Smajo Malkoc returned from working in Austria to Jezero, a village surrounding a lake, in the former Yugoslavia. He had an unusual gift for his teenaged sons Dzevad and Catib: an aquarium with two goldfish.

Two years passed. War broke out, and Smajo Malkoc was killed.

When his wife, Fehima, sneaked back into the destroyed village to bury her husband, she spotted the fish in the aquarium. She let them out into the nearby lake. "This way they might be more fortunate than us," she recalls thinking.

Fast-forward to 1995. Fehima returned with her sons to Jezero to find ruins. Eyes misting over, she turned toward the lake and glimpsed something strange. She came closer – and caught her breath.

"The whole lake was shining from the golden fish in it," she said. During the years of war and killing all around the lake, life underwater had flourished.

After their return, Fehima and her sons started feeding the fish and then selling them. Now, homes, bars, and coffee shops in the region have aquariums containing fish from Jezero.

The Malkoc house, rebuilt from ruins, is one of the biggest in the village. The family says it has enough money not to have to worry about the future.

Other residents are welcome to catch and sell the fish. But most leave that to the Malkocs. "They threw the fish into the lake," said a villager. "It's their miracle."

B Put the events in order.

_____ a. Mrs. Malkoc put the fish in a lake.

_____ b. The war broke out.

_____ c. The Malkoc family began caring for and feeding the fish in the lake.

_____ d. The Malkocs rebuilt their house.

_____ e. Mrs. Malkoc and the children returned to their home.

_____ f. Mr. Malkoc was killed.

_____ g. The Malkoc family began selling the fish.

_____ h. Mrs. Malkoc returned to the village.

__1__ i. Smajo Malkoc brought two goldfish home for his children.

Language

LESSON A · Communication skills

1

grammar

Circle the words that best complete the sentences.

1. This candidate wants to be a legislator. He (*has tried*)/ *has been tried* to get elected five times.

2. He thinks government should let private businesses run the army. When he *explained* / *was explained* this position, half of the people started yelling.

3. When he said that the government *should tax* / *should be taxed* the people more, the other half started shouting.

4. If the microphone had not broken, his speech *might have delivered* / *might have been delivered* more successfully.

5. After the microphone stopped working, everyone *cheered* / *were cheered*.

6. The audience *offered* / *was offered* a chance to ask questions, but no one did.

7. Most voters think that this candidate *will defeat* / *will be defeated* in the election – again!

2

grammar

Rewrite each sentence using the passive voice. Do not include the agent.

1. After the soccer team won the championship, the coach thanked the players.
   The players were thanked after the soccer team won the championship.

2. People have told me that I have good presentation skills.
   I have been told that I have good presentation skills

3. Schools should teach foreign languages beginning in elementary school.
   foreign languages should be taught beginning in elementary

4. The language that people hear on the street these days is full of slang.
   The language that is heard on the street these days is full of slang

5. Someone was interviewing the best-selling author on TV.
   The best-selling author was interviewed on TV

vocabulary

Rewrite the sentences by replacing the underlined words with a word or phrase from the box. If there are two possibilities, write them.

1 first	3 furthermore	5 in conclusion	7 nevertheless	9 similarly	11 to sum up
2 first of all	4 in addition	6 likewise	8 second	10 to begin	12 yet

1. <u>To start with</u>, thank you for coming to the first annual Working Moms Conference.

   To begin / First of all, thank you for coming to the first annual
   Working Moms Conference.

2. Many working moms are very busy. <u>Also</u>, many working moms are very tired!

   3, 4, 8, 9

3. We work hard to care for our families. <u>In the same manner</u>, we work hard at our jobs.

   9, 6

4. Raising kids and working is a privilege. <u>However</u>, you should take care of yourself too.

   1, 7

5. Here are some tips. <u>Before anything else</u>, take ten minutes a day to breathe and relax.

   1, 7, 10

6. <u>Next</u>, remember you don't have to solve everyone's problems!

   8

7. <u>To conclude</u>, enjoy the resources being offered today at the Working Moms Conference.

   5, 11

grammar

Complete the sentences with your own ideas. Use the passive.

1. My best friend was awarded first prize in a local photography contest.

2. Everyone was looking at me _____ when I turned the radio up too loud in the car.

3. My friend is embarrassed when _____ I talk too much while watching a movie.

4. I was being affected _____ when I ate really spicy food !

5. A child should be rewarded _____ for being a kind person.

writing

A Read the two positions about using Internet sources as references in written assignments or work presentations. Then find the supporting reasons for each position, and write them in the blanks.

Positions

1. Internet sources are trustworthy and should be used.

   _____

   _____

   _____

2. Internet sources are unreliable and shouldn't be used.

   _____

   _____

   _____

Reasons

- Internet sources can be intentionally misleading and contain false information.
- Internet sources are more convenient to research than books in libraries.
- Internet sources can suddenly disappear with no explanation.
- Internet sources usually contain more up-to-date information than books.
- Internet sources can be summaries of lengthier articles, leaving important information out.
- Internet sources are fair and balanced, providing knowledgeable information.

B Which position is closest to your position? Write a persuasive composition to explain your point of view. Be sure to argue against the opposing view.

   _____

   _____

   _____

   _____

   _____

   _____

grammar

Circle the correct form of the verbs in the paragraph. Sometimes more than one answer is correct.

Some experts in communication (1) *was /were* asked about e-mail and how it is being used today. They say that everyone who (2) *uses / use* e-mail realizes that a special style has evolved for this medium. While some writers of e-mail write in a formal style, the majority (3) *chooses /choose* a very informal style. In fact, a lot of informal messages (4) *is /are* almost conversational in style. E-mail messages may also include abbreviations that not everyone (5) *understands / understand*. A lot of younger users (6) *tend /tends* to write with abbreviations such as "IDK" for "I don't know." Only a minority of e-mail writers (7) *includes /include* customary formulas, such as "Dear Mr. Smith" and "Sincerely yours." The experts (8) *feels /feel* that a very informal style is appropriate for business e-mail.

grammar

Read these results from a student survey. Then use the words in the box to make statements. Use each word only once.

Why do you study a foreign language?	
	Percentage of students
1. I expect to get a better job.	85%
2. I want to use the language for travel.	100%
3. I have to because it's a required subject.	30%
4. I need to be able to read literature in the language.	0%
5. I do it just for fun.	50%

| all | half | majority | minority | none |

1. want to use the language for travel

   All of the students want to use the language for travel.

2. do it just for fun

   _____

3. expect to get a better job

   _____

4. need to be able to read literature in the language

   _____

5. have to because it's a required subject

   _____

3

vocabulary

Complete the dialogues by using the correct form of the expressions in the box. Make any necessary changes.

have a sharp tongue
have a way with words
love to hear oneself talk
stick to the point
talk behind someone's back
talk someone into something
talk someone's ear off

1. A: I really liked what Joe said about working together as a team.

   B: I agree. It was very inspiring. He really __has a way with words__ .

2. A: Did Peter say anything about me after I left?

   B: No. He'd never _____ . He'd tell you directly.

3. A: Did you tell Lisa about our plans for her birthday?

   B: I tried to, but she just kept _____ about her problems with her car.

4. A: Ms. Chao read my report and said awful things about it.

   B: Well, she _____ , but she's also very perceptive. Just try to focus on what she's saying about your work.

5. A: I know you want to discuss the report, but I want to talk about my new customer.

   B: Let's _____ . We can talk about that later.

6. A: That meeting was so long! I thought Bob would never stop talking!

   B: He sure _____ , doesn't he?

7. A: Are you going to the company picnic this weekend?

   B: Well, I wasn't planning to, but Kelly convinced me to go. She knows how to _____ I don't want to do!

4

grammar

Complete these sentences with your own ideas.

1. Each language in the world _is unique._ _____

2. All bilingual people _____

   _____

3. Every one of my classmates _____

   _____

4. The majority of TV newscasters _____

   _____

5

reading

A Read the article. Find the words in boldface that match these definitions.

1. obstacle ___impediment___
2. the existing state of affairs _____
3. strongly disapproving of _____
4. value, worth _____
5. justification _____

Dialects

Do you hold any of the following beliefs?

- There is a single standard variety of American English.
- Varieties of English that differ from the standard are substandard.
- Official encouragement of more than one language is an **impediment** to national unity.

All of these beliefs about language are widely held. Nearly everyone has an opinion about language. Examining what people believe about language, scholars say, allows us to identify deeper impulses, such as fear of the unfamiliar, language "standards" as a way of preserving the social **status quo**, and criticizing "substandard" speech as a coded expression of prejudice.

Judged on purely linguistic grounds, all languages and dialects have equal **merit**. All come from the same human cognitive faculties; all have the same expressive potential; all operate according to the same kinds of logical systems. Why, then, are some dialects considered substandard? The answer is simple: Judgments about relative worth are socially determined.

Many people believe there is a single standard American English dialect, but in reality, no one dialect exists. "If you said to anyone, 'Here's a room; put the hundred people in there you think speak the best English,' you'd get people that speak all different kinds of English," says the linguist Rosina Lippi-Green.

According to Lippi-Green, the myth of one standard dialect helps us to keep out the ones that are uncomfortable to us. This provides a **rationale** for preserving the existing social order, or **condemning** others for their "broken" language.

B Read these statements. Are they supported by the information in the article? Check (✓) yes or no.

	Yes	No
1. There is one standard variety of American English.	☐	☐
2. Some languages are inferior in terms of the expressiveness and logic.	☐	☐
3. Criticizing the kind of language that a person uses is sometimes a substitute for criticizing that person's social group.	☐	☐

1 grammar

Rewrite these sentences using compound adjectives. More than one answer is possible.

1. Nicole is a model with curly hair and brown eyes.

   Nicole is a curly-haired, brown-eyed model.

2. In my opinion, the politician's speech was too long.

   _____

3. I was confused by the salesperson, who was talking very fast.

   _____

4. Maxwell's is not a restaurant that many people know about.

   _____

5. The famous conductor is recognized by many people.

   _____

6. Dr. Kendall is a professor who really makes us think about things.

   _____

7. Katy made a good impression at the interview because she was dressed so well.

   _____

2 vocabulary

Circle the words that best complete the sentences.

1. The (coolheaded) / soft-hearted athlete was able to score despite the noisy crowd.
2. My *absent-minded / hardheaded* professor had scheduled an exam for today, but he forgot to bring the exams to class!
3. Sam is the kindest and most *cold-blooded / warm-hearted* guy I know.
4. Although Emily appears to be silly and *narrow-minded / empty-headed*, she's actually quite intelligent.
5. Roy is *hardheaded / hot-blooded*. Once he makes up his mind, he doesn't change.
6. I hope Zach is *cold-hearted / open-minded* about our idea. He isn't always willing to consider new approaches to solving problems.
7. My parents are so *narrow-minded / soft-hearted* when it comes to music. They won't listen to anything except jazz.
8. The *cold-hearted / absent-minded* killer was sentenced to life in prison.

grammar

What qualities should these people have? Write a sentence using two compound adjectives.

elementary school teacher

1. An elementary school teacher should be kind-hearted and well educated.

mountain climber

2. _____

    _____

    _____

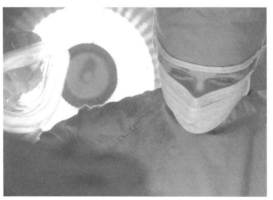

surgeon

3. _____

    _____

    _____

judge

4. _____

    _____

    _____

car salesman

5. _____

    _____

    _____

soccer player

6. _____

    _____

    _____

4

writing

A Read this biography of composer and conductor Leonard Bernstein. Then answer the questions below.

LEONARD BERNSTEIN

LEONARD BERNSTEIN was perhaps the single greatest figure in American classical music in the twentieth century. Born in 1918 in Lawrence, Massachusetts, he studied piano as a child in Boston. **1** Upon his graduation from Harvard in 1939, he went to Philadelphia to study at the Curtis Institute. **2** By the time Bernstein finished his training, he was widely respected as a major talent in the music world. **3**

In 1943, Bernstein became the assistant conductor of the New York Philharmonic. One night, he was asked to substitute for a conductor who was sick. This was a particularly difficult concert, but Bernstein performed brilliantly and was a great success. **4** Over the next 15 years, he held conducting positions in several of the great orchestras of the world, and he performed as a guest conductor with many others. His work included both live concerts and recordings. **5**

In 1958, Bernstein became the music director of the New York Philharmonic. That same year, he started a series of televised programs called *Young People's Concerts*, designed to teach children an appreciation for great music. At the Philharmonic, Bernstein was a very popular conductor. He brought new music to the orchestra, and he revitalized older music that hadn't been played for some time.

6 Bernstein died in New York City in 1990. He was conducting and composing music up until the time of his death. Through his lifetime of conducting, composing, teaching, and helping people understand music, he left a great gift to the world.

1. In what year did Leonard Bernstein leave Harvard University? _____

2. How long did Bernstein conduct orchestras all over the world before he became the music director of the New York Philharmonic? _____

3. In what year did Bernstein start *Young People's Concerts*? _____

B There are six boxes in the biography. Find where each of the following sentences should go and write the number of the box beside the sentence.

_____ a. In 1969, Bernstein left the New York Philharmonic and spent the remaining years of his life composing a wide variety of music, conducting all over the world, and teaching young musicians.

_____ b. At 17, he entered Harvard University, where he studied composition.

_____ c. During his years there, he spent his summers at the Boston Symphony Orchestra's institute at Tanglewood, where he studied with the conductor Serge Koussevitzky.

C Choose someone you admire who has made a difference in people's lives. Research the key facts of the person's life, and write a three-paragraph biography.

grammar 1

Read the text and underline the superlative compound adjectives.

Without a doubt, my <u>most fondly remembered</u> teacher was Mr. Hill, my college French professor. He was the most kind-hearted man, and he always showed concern for his students. He went out of his way to make us feel comfortable in class, so we never felt nervous or anxious. He was the hardest-working teacher I've ever had, which made it easy to learn. When he taught us to speak, he was very good. He truly loved French culture, so the cultural lessons were the most thought-provoking. He made me feel that I was looking through a window into another world, and he made me want to be a part of that world. I guess I never learned much French – it's not the most easily acquired language – but I did learn how good a teacher can be and how rewarding it can be to learn about another culture.

grammar 2

Read these dialogues and fill in the blank with the superlative form of the adjectives in parentheses.

1. Kay: What did you think about the president's speech?

   Mindy: I thought it was <u>the most thought-provoking</u> (thought-provoking) speech she's ever given.

2. Sung: Don't you think Tom is lazy?

   Nate: Well, he's definitely not _____ (hard-working) person I know!

3. Oscar: What did you think of the lead actor's performance in the movie we saw last night?

   Valerie: I thought he was terrific. He gave one of _____ (heartbreakingly convincing) performances in the movie.

4. Rich: Have you seen the video clip of the singing dog on the Internet?

   Linda: No, I haven't. But I've heard that it's one of _____ (widely downloaded) clips of the week.

5. Tai: I heard that Cory was chosen to be manager of the new design project.

   Sarah: That doesn't surprise me. Cory is one of _____ (highly respected) people in our department.

6. Brad: How was your trip to Morocco? Were you able to visit the desert?

   Nora: Oh, I did. It was one of _____ (breathtakingly beautiful) things I saw on my entire trip!

grammar

Rewrite the sentences to make them true for you.
If the sentence is already true for you, write a sentence
to support your opinion. Use superlative compound
adjectives in your sentences.

1. The most talented actor I can think of is
   Hugh Jackman.

   I agree. Hugh Jackman is one of the
   most talented actors I've ever seen!

2. The most action-packed movie I've ever seen is
   Lord of the Rings.

   _____

3. The most time-saving invention is the
   microwave oven.

   _____

4. The most easily learned language is English.

   _____

Hugh Jackman

5. In my opinion, the spiciest food is from Korea.

   _____

6. Basketball is the most physically demanding sport I know.

   _____

vocabulary

Correct the underlined mistake in each sentence with one of the words in the box.
Some words will be used more than once.

after	on	to	through	with

1. I always look <u>through</u> my older sister for fashion advice. ____to____
2. Sometimes you need to go <u>after</u> hard times to appreciate what you have. _____
3. I'm not sure who to side <u>to</u> in this argument! You both have valid points. _____
4. Many middle-aged people not only look <u>with</u> their children, but they take care of their
   elderly parents at the same time. _____
5. Who do you take <u>through</u> more, your mother or your father? _____
6. I have very high expectations for myself, and I get annoyed with myself when I don't
   live up <u>on</u> them. _____
7. Excuse me while I check <u>after</u> the baby. I think I just heard her cry. _____
8. If you don't face up <u>with</u> your problems soon, they'll only get worse. _____

5 reading

A Read this article about Médecins Sans Frontières (MSF), or Doctors Without Borders. Then check the adjectives that describe the organization.

- ☐ 1. Oslo-based
- ☐ 2. overly bureaucratic
- ☐ 3. award-winning
- ☐ 4. narrow-minded
- ☐ 5. internationally minded

DISTINGUISHED SERVICE

Shortly before the winner of the 1999 Nobel Peace Prize was announced, staffers at the Paris headquarters of Médecins Sans Frontières – Doctors Without Borders – played down their chances. "We've been nominated so many times already," said one, "but we're always passed over." Not this time. The Oslo-based Nobel committee named the crusading medical and humanitarian organization as its newest peace laureate.

The committee's statement praised the 28-year-old group for its "pioneering humanitarian work on several continents" and for championing "the fundamental principle that all disaster victims, whether the disaster is natural or human in origin, have a right to professional assistance given as quickly and efficiently as possible." The prestigious $975,000 award was quite a recompense for what started as a ragtag band of antiestablishment French doctors. It has since grown into an international network with 23 offices, fielding 2,000 medical volunteers in 80 countries and commanding an annual budget of $167 million – nearly 80 percent of which comes from private donations.

MSF has always asserted its independence from governments or large bureaucratic organizations like the International Red Cross. In fact, it was created largely as a reaction to the Red Cross approach of strict neutrality and respect for diplomatic niceties. "International relief agencies were too respectful of notions of noninterference and sovereignty," recalls MSF co-founder Rony Brauman. "When we saw people dying on the other side of the frontiers, we asked ourselves, 'What is this border? It doesn't mean anything to us.'"

While the Red Cross would only enter a crisis zone with local government permission and forbade its volunteers and staffers to side with any political entity, the founders of MSF were activists who insisted on a "duty to interfere" in troubled areas and to speak out about what they saw. "The movement was political from the start," explained co-founder Bernard Kouchner. "The tradition was medical, the action was medical, but we had to convince people that borders should not protect disgraceful conduct and suffering."

B Check (✓) whether each statement applies to MSF or to the Red Cross.

	MSF	Red Cross
1. It started with a small, informal group of doctors.	☐	☐
2. It received the Nobel Peace Prize in 1999.	☐	☐
3. It pays attention to diplomatic concerns.	☐	☐
4. It waits for local governments' permission before entering crisis zones.	☐	☐
5. It tries to make political points.	☐	☐

Business matters

LESSON A · Entrepreneurs

vocabulary

Circle the words that best complete the sentences.

1. I would rather work *around* / *for* a boss who is organized and strict instead of a boss who is disorganized and nice.

2. Before Jo started his business, he worked *off* / *on* the balance on his student loans.

3. Showing up late for appointments can work *against* / *toward* you if you are trying to start a new business.

4. If we don't find a way to work *toward* / *around* this problem, we'll never make our deadline.

5. The more people we have working *for* / *on* the report, the faster we'll get it done!

6. Jesse is working *off* / *toward* a degree in marketing and finance.

grammar

Read each sentence and then answer the questions with *yes* or *no*.

Had Janet not lost her job at a bakery, she would never have considered starting her own business.

1. Did Janet lose her job at the bakery? _____Yes_____

2. Did she consider starting her own business? _____

Were she to have known how difficult running her own business would be, she probably wouldn't have started one.

3. Did she know how difficult a business would be? _____

4. Did she start a business? _____

Had Janet had a large family, she might not have been able to spend a lot of time developing her business.

5. Was she able to spend a lot of time developing the business? _____

6. Did she have a large family? _____

Janet's Cookies might not have become the best-selling cookies in the city had she not worked so hard.

7. Did Janet's Cookies become the best-selling cookies in the city? _____

8. Did Janet work hard? _____

grammar

Write a sentence for each situation using a conditional clause (*Had . . . not . . .*).

1. __Had__ the woman __not answered the ad__ , she would never have become a veterinarian assistant.

2. _____ the man _____ , he wouldn't have won first prize.

3. _____ the woman _____ , she wouldn't have started her own business.

4. _____ the couple _____ , they wouldn't have had all the kittens.

5. _____ the woman _____ , she wouldn't have bought her new computer.

6. _____ the man _____ , he would never have been waited on.

4

writing

A Read this business letter. Three sentences do not belong because they are too personal or irrelevant. Cross them out.

85 Sun Road
Phoenix, AZ 85051

Ms. Rosa Marquez
Quick Copy Center
4226 N. 22nd St.
Phoenix, AZ 85016

June 7, 2009

Dear Ms. Marquez:

I am writing in response to the advertisement for a copy machine technician in last Sunday's Phoenix *Star*. I am very interested in the position and am enclosing my résumé for your consideration. It is very kind of you to read this letter.

I believe that I meet all of the qualifications that you specify. You have probably never had a candidate as qualified as I am! I have had five years of experience as a copy machine technician in a retail environment. I am trained in digital and color technology, and I have experience with all major brands of equipment.

In addition to my technical skills, I enjoy training staff members and am very good with customers. None of my current customers wants me to leave.

I would appreciate the opportunity to discuss this position with you in person. I look forward to hearing from you at your convenience.

Sincerely,

James Ditzler

James Ditzler

B Imagine a job that you would be interested in having. Make notes on the following.

Why you want the position:

_____

_____

Your experience:

_____

_____

Why you should be considered:

_____

_____

C Use your notes to write a business letter applying for the job you are interested in.

grammar

Match the clauses to make conditional sentences.

1. Assuming that I was required to travel for my job, _d_

2. On the condition that your company paid for part of it, _____

3. Provided that an applicant had the right job skills, _____

4. Supposing that your boss wanted to transfer you to a different department, _____

5. Whether or not you have a good reason to change jobs, _____

a. I'd consider hiring him or her.

b. I'd strongly recommend staying at your present company.

c. how would you feel about it?

d. I would turn it down because I don't like to fly.

e. would you go back to school in the evenings?

grammar

Respond to what the first speaker says in the conversations. Write sentences using the adverb clauses of condition provided.

1. A: If I were offered an interesting job that paid well, I would accept it. (provided that)

   B: _I would probably accept it too, provided that the_ _benefits were also good._

2. A: If I had to commute to work on a daily basis, I would definitely do it. It can't be that much of an inconvenience. (on the condition that)

   B: _____

   _____

3. A: If I didn't receive a raise within the first year I worked at a job, I'd leave it and find a new one. (assuming that)

   B: _____

   _____

4. A: Under no circumstances would I ever accept a demotion. No one should move down in a company. (supposing that)

   B: _____

   _____

5. A: If my boss said something in a meeting that I strongly disagreed with, I would definitely speak up. (whether or not)

   B: _____

   _____

6. A: I think that it's okay to lend a family member a large amount of money in order to start a business. (provided that)

   B: _____

   _____

3

grammar

Under what conditions would you do or not do these things? Write sentences using the expressions in the box.

assuming (that)
on the condition (that)
provided (that)
supposing (that)
whether or not

1. take a pay cut

   I'd take a pay cut on the condition I was given more interesting projects
   at work.

2. work every weekend

3. be transferred to a different country

4. work two jobs at the same time

5. quit your job and go back to school

4

vocabulary

Choose the quality that you consider to be the most important for each job.
Then write a sentence explaining why.

1. doctor (leadership ability / training)

   Training is most important for doctors because people's lives are in their hands.

2. artist (self-discipline / initiative)

3. politician (charisma / influence)

4. teacher (communication skills / leadership ability)

5. writer (initiative / training)

6. business executive (influence / leadership ability)

5
reading

A Read the article. What do you think the prefix *bio-* means? _____

NEW RECRUITMENT PROCEDURES

Traditional recruiting procedures for attracting high-quality workers include background checks and face-to-face interviews. However, some employers are augmenting the usual screening methods with less conventional techniques. Although these procedures are used to weed out undesirable applicants, they also help to assess potential.

Reading minds and muscles

Although most tests assess behavioral patterns, others – such as biofeedback – are being used to evaluate injuries on the job. Biofeedback, which assesses impulses from the brain to the muscles, can determine the validity of an injury and therefore the legitimacy of an insurance claim. The procedure also can detect vulnerabilities in people who are prone to injuries.

Handwriting analysis

Debbie Berk, president of Signature Dynamics, a handwriting-analysis firm, says that 90 percent of her clients are managers seeking either to assess work potential or to analyze the behavior of current employees. Although many people balk at using this method, it has been used to determine promotions or new hires at many companies. "I've had clients tell me they thought this was voodoo," Berk said. "But they have seen the validity in it and continue to use my services."

Watchdogs

Companies do not use these methods without oversight. Civil rights lawyers track both traditional and nontraditional screening procedures and file charges opposing those that appear to be discriminatory. Massachusetts, for example, now outlaws psychological testing in employee screening. Lawyers have also argued that some tests contain questions irrelevant to job performance.

Insights

Many agree that one of the oldest recruitment methods – the interview – is the still the best. The psychologist Vivian Lord has studied workplace behavior extensively. She notes that the best personality indicators are in the answers to an interviewer's questions. Consider the questions below and what the response (in parentheses) is meant to show.

- "Describe the best boss you ever had. Describe the worst boss you ever had." (Does the person claim "personality conflicts" to explain problems?)

- "Tell me about a failure in your life and why it occurred." (Does he or she take responsibility – or blame others?)

- "Describe a problem you had in which someone else's help was important to you." (Does he or she give the person credit or express appreciation?)

No one method works for every company. In order to recruit the best employees, a manager must choose screening procedures that reveal the behaviors most sought after – and most necessary to avoid – for his or her own department. The good news is, there are many to choose from.

B According to the information in the article, the following sentences are false. Rewrite them to make them true.

1. Biofeedback is used to determine how intelligent job applicants are.

   _____

2. Handwriting analysis is widely accepted as a useful tool in assessing job candidates.

   _____

3. Lawyers never find unfairness in companies' recruitment practices.

   _____

4. The traditional interview is no longer considered to be a useful recruitment method.

   _____